Confident, Calm and Clutch

How to Build Confidence and Mental Toughness for Young Athletes Using Sports Psychology

Valerie R. Alston MA CMPC

Alchemy Publishing Group LLC

Copyright © 2023 by Alchemy Publishing Group

The content within this book may not be reproduced, duplicated or transmitted without direct written permission from the author or the publisher.

Under no circumstances will any blame or legal responsibility be held against the publisher, or author, for any damages, reparation, or monetary loss due to the information contained within this book. Either directly or indirectly. You are responsible for your own choices, actions, and results.

Legal Notice:

This book is copyright protected. This book is only for personal use. You cannot amend, distribute, sell, use, quote or paraphrase any part, of the content within this book, without the consent of the author or publisher.

Disclaimer Notice:

Please note the information contained within this document is for educational and entertainment purposes only. All effort has been expended to present accurate, up-to-date, and reliable, complete information. No warranties of any kind are declared or implied. Readers acknowledge that the author is not engaging in the rendering of legal, financial, medical or professional advice. The content within this book has been derived from various sources. Please consult a licensed professional before attempting any techniques outlined in this book.

By reading this document, the reader agrees that under no circumstances is the author responsible for any losses, direct or indirect, which are incurred as a result of the use of the information contained within this document, including, but not limited to, — errors, omissions, or inaccuracies.

Contents

Free Gift For Readers — III

Introduction — 1

1. Special Note to Parents of Young Athletes — 7
2. Skill 1: Mental Toughess Myths — 13
3. Skill 2: How to Control Your Emotions — 19
4. Skill 3: How to Improve Consistency — 29
5. Skill 4: How to Build Your Champion Support Team — 37
6. Skill 5: How to Build Your Inner Strength — 45
7. Skill 6: How to Exercise Your Way to Mental Toughness — 55
8. Skill 7: How to Set Goals the Right Way — 61
9. Quick Fix Mental Skills You Can Use Now — 71
10. How to Fix Common Problems — 77
11. Conclusion — 83
12. Additional Resources — 89

Index — 97

Coaches Corner — 99

A Free Gift To Readers

Get access to the Athletic Coping Skills Inventory. Discover how you score on 7 key areas of mental toughness that impact your athletic performance. Use the link to discover your score today!

https://valstoncoaching.typeform.com/ACSIscore

Introduction

My high school team had a magical playoff run during my sophomore year. We were in the state championship softball game. I led the team in hits and RBI throughout the playoffs. My home run in the semi-final game propelled us into the big game. I entered the batter's box with two runners on. A base hit would have broken the game open.

Then something strange happened. I couldn't breathe. I couldn't relax. My mind started racing. My shoulders felt tight and I couldn't get comfortable. I fouled off two pitches I should have hammered. Then I watched the 3rd strike without swinging. I struck out, stranding the runners in scoring position. We ended up losing the game 2-1 against a team we had the talent to beat. I had let myself and my team down. That failure bothered me for months.

Fast forward to the end of my Junior year. We made it to the state championship game once again. I came up in the 7th inning of a tie game with the winning run on second base. I was ready. Earlier in the game, I had driven an inside pitch into the right center gap. The pitcher refused to throw me an inside pitch during this at bat. We battled hard. I fouled off 8 straight two strike pitches and on pitch number nine; I took a mighty swing... and struck out again. My response to that strikeout as a junior differed from the previous year. I was confident and remained calm. And I knew I would not fail if I got another chance.

At the bottom of the 10th inning, the game remained tied. A runner was on first base. On the first pitch of the at bat she pitched me up and away again. I drove the ball off the left field wall for a game winning double (it could have been a triple but by the time I got to 2nd base my teammate had scored so I made a slight detour towards home plate to dog pile on her instead). Yes, it was outstanding winning the state championship. More importantly for this story, it proved that my recent training with my sport psychologist worked. And it led me to choose this path for my career.

Baseball and softball are both games of failure. Hitters will fail more than they succeed. I was the same size, strength and person as a sophomore. During my junior season, I became Confident, Calm and Clutch.

Here is the shocking truth about competitive athletes. All the physical skills in the world don't guarantee success. Less talented athletes can beat more talented athletes because they are mentally tougher. Athletes who can't get out of their heads will struggle.

I was never the best athlete on any team I played on. Through mental toughness, I hit and defended well. I succeeded with mental quickness rather than foot speed. My mindset helped me go from being an all county high school catcher from a small Christian High School to the starting second baseman for the University of Minnesota for four years.

This book is about how **you** can improve your athletic success by mastering the mental skills necessary to compete at a high level. I know you can do it because I did it. Several travel ball coaches told me I was too small or too slow to play on their team. Several told me I was too slow to play second base in college. And yet, I became one of the best fielding second baseman in the Big Ten conference because I possessed mental toughness and understood how to maximize my own strengths. I refused to accept the limitations others attempted to impose on me.

The parent of a high school athlete who is a five star recruit every coach wants has an enormous opportunity. I hope you will read this book to make sure your child gets the most out of their talent by learning the right mental approach to thrive.

If your child is **NOT** an all-star recruit, then you should read this book to help your child overcome their supposed limitations. Coaches prefer average talent with a great mindset over superior talent with a bad mindset any day.

This book is for high school players who want to perform better, whether they are trying to be recruited or not.

College coaches recruit talent and everyone knows who the super gifted athletes are. But 80% of the players in college sports are not super gifted. They outwork and out think their competition to get where they are.

Mental toughness is important for any athlete, but it is essential for athletes with less physical talent than the superstars. Only 5% of high school players are the superstars every college coach wants. The rest of us have to work harder and play smarter to earn our scholarship or spot on the team.

The Shocking Truth

Every competitive high school sport requires hours of practice to master the game skills. Few high school or travel ball coaches have the certification to help you master the mental toughness skills needed to perform at the highest levels of your sport.

If you will not receive mental skills training from your coaches, then you must take it upon yourself to read this book so you can become the best version of yourself. Imagine..

- Feeling strong and confident on the field
- Overcoming an error and make a brilliant play on your next attempt
- Performing at your best in the clutch moments that matter.
- Getting better everyday throughout your season/career.
- Playing with joy and enthusiasm every day because you focus on the right things.

- Performing at the peak of your abilities every time you take the field, court, or pitch.

- Receiving multiple scholarship offers to pay for your college education.

I achieved these things because I was lucky enough to learn the sport psychology techniques and mental skills to maximize my athletic skills while I was still in high school. You can learn these skills as well.

A lack of confidence or refined mental process often derails performance. If you build the right processes, you will build the right level of confidence. The performance gap between a confident athlete and an athlete that doubts themselves is enormous.

This book will help you discover the 7 mental skills needed to perform at the highest level in your sport:

- Understand what mental toughness is, and why it is important.

- Regulate your emotions by managing your thoughts and actions in productive ways.

- Build your Coachability by taking responsibility for your thoughts, emotions, and actions.

- Develop a support system that will remove negativity from your life.

- Compound your strengths through self-care and effective thinking.

- Appreciate and use exercise and physical training as a tool in mental toughness.

- Step outside of your comfort zone and move towards thriving in sport and life.

And if you are a parent reading this book, I will provide you with some tips about how to help your teen overcome the mental hurdles to their success. Unfortunately, misguided but well-intentioned parental pressure can make the problem worse, rather than better. If you and your child are on the same page, you will thrive.

My favorite quote of all time is by Yogi Berra, the Hall of Fame catcher for the New York Yankees. He said, "90% of the game is half-mental." And I think he was right!

My tournament fast-pitch softball career began in Southern California when I was 8 years old. I was the youngest kid on the team. Over the next 10 years, I played over 1000 travel ball games because we played 48 weekends a year. My teams competed at the ASA softball nationals every year. (ASA was where all the top players in the country competed.)

I earned a BS in kinesiology from the University of Minnesota in 2006 and my Master's degree in Mental Health and Sport Psychology from Boston University in 2008. As a Certified Mental Performance Consultant with the Association of Applied Sport Psychology and a trained Health and Wellness Coach from the Functional Medicine Coaching Academy (FMCA), I work with a variety of clients.

Since 2008, I have been a Mental Skills Trainer for the United States Army working with Soldiers. The skills we help them develop matter in life or death situations. I teach them to remain calm under pressure, to focus on what they can control, and to persevere against all odds. For my Soldiers, these skills can mean the difference between surviving the battle or not, saving lives or not, making it through an important Army school or not.

The human brain is an amazing device. It is also the root cause of performance failures when it gets in your way of doing what you need to do to perform. Sport situations are not usually life or death, but your brain can respond like it is. The huge spike of hormones and counterproductive changes in your body prevent you from getting into the zone. It impedes your ability to perform under pressure, which needs to be done to excel and thrive. In the championship game, I struck out when I had the ability not to. The difference between failure and success is understanding how to apply specific mental toughness techniques.

The fight-or-flight response is a biochemical reaction to stress. Stress causes a physiological reaction that prevents smooth fluid muscle motion. Left unchecked, the muscles tighten and do not respond as you need them to.

In my work, I help Soldiers not just survive, but also thrive under stressful and sometimes life-threatening conditions. I have played sports my whole life, have struggled and failed, competed and succeeded. I have overcome my physical limitations to play the game better than superior athletes born with more talent.

I can help you become a better performing athlete. Most youth coaching focuses on the mechanics of physical skills, with little time spent on mental training. The greatest improvement in your play and enjoyment of your chosen game will happen when you develop the right mental skills to become a Confident, Calm and Clutch athlete.

This book will help you build the foundational skills needed to become Confident, Calm and Clutch.

If you still aren't sure whether you need this book, take this short quiz called the Athlete Skills Coping Skill Inventory for free on my website. This scientifically validated instrument will score you on the key areas of mental toughness. If you score low on any of the items, this book will help you overcome your deficiencies!

Valerie Alston, MA, CMPC . "Enhance your performance, Enhance your Life"

Chapter One
Special Note to Parents of Young Athletes

Many parents secretly wish their child would be the star of the game. You want them to win the game for their team. You want them to excel at their sport. And it's pretty exhilarating to brag about your budding star when you get back to work after the big game. However, no parent wants to cause their young athlete's failure. Unfortunately, one of the biggest reasons young athletes at elite levels quit their sport is because of the significant amount of pressure placed on them by parents and coaches.

Research suggests that parents (particularly fathers) may not perceive their own behaviors as exerting pressure on their child. Performance experts agree that children who perceive parental pressure are likely to experience competitive anxiety and sport burnout (Kanters & Casper, 2008). The number one reason kids quit a sport is because it is no longer fun. They started playing the game because it was fun, and when it was no longer fun, they move on to something else.

The pressure on young athletes has mushroomed with the "pay to play" model. Sports like baseball, basketball, hockey, gymnastics, volleyball and soccer demand young kids specialize in their sport earlier and earlier if they want to succeed. As a parent, I know you love your child and you want what's best for them. So here are some simple tips to avoid putting pressure on your child that might cause them to stop having fun, underperform, or even quit.

Parental Tip Number One

Every young athlete who wants to play their sport at an elite level needs to receive high-quality coaching when they are young to learn the fundamentals of the sport. Don't focus on playtime, focus on coaching and skill development. If they receive good coaching, they will get better. Assure your child that they will get to play when they work hard to refine their skills. If you focus on selecting a team based on the amount of play time they get, you may hurt their long-term success. So be careful of your motivations when you select a team.

Parental Tip Number Two

If you become a coach for your child's team, it is essential that you award playtime based on performance and not on nepotism. Your child should understand the need to earn their playtime. If they don't, they will be missing an important life lesson and their progress will stall. Very little in adulthood is given. Jobs, pay raises, opportunities must be earned. If your child learns how to work hard and earn their way onto the field, the hope is that they will be better equipped to earn opportunities as an adult.

Parental Tip Number Three

The process of success is more important than outcomes. Focusing on outcomes leads parents to being excited when their child gets a base hit and disappointed when they make an out. This can put pressure on your athlete to break one of the cardinal rules of performance enhancement, which is to control what you can control.

There is a correct way to approach and execute any athletic skill. Doing the skill right will lead to more success. Reward the correct approach and process and your child will improve. Focus only on the outcome and your player may get discouraged and fail. No matter what sport your child plays, applying the right effort or strategies and executing skills properly will go better for them in the long run. If they prepare well and use the right processes, they will set conditions for excellence.

Actual outcomes (wins, losses, batting average, touchdowns, goals scored) are often outside of their control. The right processes will help an athlete improve faster. Your goal needs to be understanding their process and helping them do it correctly. The right preparation, effort, skills and strategy should be rewarded. Focusing only on outcomes can be a disincentive to preparation. Parental displeasure when their young athlete cannot get the outcome you both want can undermine progress towards mental toughness. Make sure that your kid knows that your love and affection are not dependent on their results.

Parental Tip Number Four

Resist comparing your child to other kids in the sport. Your child has his/her own strengths and deficiencies. Discuss your child's strengths and weaknesses. Work with coaches to identify needed improvements. Help them with the drills. Teach your child to work hard and control what they can control. Encourage them to practice the right mechanics of movement, and they will get better. Help them see the joy in getting better and improving their craft.

Parental Tip Number Five

Read this entire book. If you still need help after you've finished the book, contact me. No two athletes have the same issues. I provide personalized coaching and tailored programs to help you, help your young athlete achieve their full potential. Kids and parents can sometimes be at odds with each other concerning sport. When that happens, a neutral third party can help break the logjam and get you back on track. I will help you if you need it. *(See the resource page for more details)*

Parental Tip Number Six

Don't tell your young athlete what to do regarding their sport. Ask them questions to uncover what they think. Some sample questions are:

"What do you want to achieve?"

"Do you want to learn how to be calm in clutch moments?"

"Would you like to reduce stress during the game?"

"What are your goals for this season?" Then listen to the answers.

This book will explain the knowledge and drills your athlete needs to become mentally tough. Help your student explore the options by reading this book together and discussing each chapter. Don't be a teller. Be the assistant, not the boss. We assume we know what is happening with them when we tell.

Parents don't attend every practice. They are often not privy to the coaching being received in real time during games/competition. It's a better practice to start by asking, than assuming. As it relates to mental toughness skills, ask them if they would like to identify the mental skills they need to work on. Then use the link in the *resource pages* to take the Athletic Coping Skill Inventory created by (Smith et al. 1994) to determine what area of mental toughness that your athlete might need to work on most and start there.

Parental Tip Number Seven

Try to care less than they do. What do I mean by that? Often parents can become more invested in their child's success in sport than their own kid.

When your goals for your child don't match what they want out of their sport, it creates a lot of conflict. It's also important to know that kids often change their mind as they grow and mature. Especially, as they reach high school, their priorities might shift, which is okay.

Maybe they don't want to work so hard to become elite. Or perhaps they found a new passion. It can cause frustration when you want something more than your child. Be mindful of whether you are still supporting them in their goals or have moved past what they want and are pushing your own goals on them.

Chapter Two
Skill 1: Mental Toughess Myths

Confident, calm and clutch are more than words in this book. These are the critical performance skills in every sport. Do you remain confident under pressure? Does your mind remain calm and free from negative thoughts during your competition? Do you make the play when it matters? Athletes who freak out from stress are not confident. They are not calm. And they are not clutch. Championship teams will face adversity during the season. Skilled players will face adversity during their season. The ability to remain confident, calm and clutch separates the average from the elite. Confident, calm and clutch players are mentally tough.

Let me explain why mental toughness is important to young athletes. I want you to imagine the following scenario. You have worked hard to develop your athletic skills. For years, you've played hundreds of games. You've gone to thousands of practices, trained your body, sacrificed your social life, and worked hard to become an elite player. You have done everything you can to be a successful athlete, hoping to be recruited for a college scholarship.

Then in your critical junior year, which is typically when colleges can talk to athletes. You have a change in coaches. Your new coach doesn't know you well, doesn't recognize the quality of your play, and decides not to play you at the important scouting tournaments throughout the summer. By the time you are at the largest exposure tournament that all college coaches attend, he has brought back college players who play your position. He reduces your role to part time on the team you helped earn a berth at nationals.

How would that make you feel? Would you think that was fair? Would your parents think your athletic career was over?

Could you manipulate this crappy situation to ensure that multiple college coaches wanted to offer you a scholarship to play the game you love?

Life always throws you a challenge. It is not the level of the challenge that defeats you; it is your response to the challenge. You cannot control what happens to you. You **can** always control how you respond to what happens.

This exact scenario happened to me. I got 7 at bats as a pinch hitter in seven games and never played in the field. How would your parents have reacted? How would you behave? Would your disappointment be obvious to observers? I will explain what happened in the next chapter when I focus on taking the best approach to overcoming adversity. But the key message for you right now is that my response and my father's response made an enormous difference to the outcome.

After barely taking part in the games, I left the tournament with 5 recruiting visits booked. I accepted a full-ride scholarship at the University of Minnesota. I became a four-year starter for the Gophers. Thousands of young players in your sport have the athletic ability to play the game in college. But far fewer have the mental toughness to achieve that goal.

This book will explain the mental toughness skills you need to be a person college coaches want to invest their precious scholarship dollars in. My personal stories show the mental side of sport throughout this book. I will explain how you can put yourself in the best position to achieve your dream of playing your sport in college. Mental skills will help you thrive in any activity.

To strengthen mental toughness, it's important to understand the concept in depth. Mental toughness is the ability to bounce back from setbacks and move forward by growing through every part of life's process (school, sport, social life, family). Struggling is a natural part of living. What matters is how we react to struggle. It is super easy to be upbeat when everything is going well. It is far more difficult when nothing goes right.

To compete in any endeavor, you can not allow failure to knock you down and keep you down. Failure is an essential building block to greatness. Anytime you think you are perfect, a competitive failure reminds you that you have more work to do to improve. Overcoming failure motivates you to get better. And regardless of the sport you play, you will fail. You will get beat, you will mess up, and you will do stupid things. No-one is perfect. As soon as you embrace failure as a reminder that you have more to learn, you will begin your journey to becoming an elite mentally tough athlete.

Mental toughness is also the ability to take calculated risks (trying something new, volunteering to go first, being willing to make a few mistakes as you learn and grow, getting out of your comfort zone, etc.). This ability translates to being able to thrive in your sport and in life. Sometimes, getting by and surviving is necessary in life, but the goal is to move you towards thriving!

Thriving means living a life of purpose and meaning. It means having positive and fulfilling relationships with parents, friends, and coaches. It means accomplishing your goals. People who thrive are more positive. People who thrive enjoy life.

Mental toughness is much like physical fitness. It will deteriorate if you don't work on it. One way I can help you understand mental toughness is to debunk some myths that you might have heard. These common myths often impede mental toughness and slow down progress:

Mental Toughness Myths

1. Myth: Tough-Minded people don't feel negative emotions. They don't get sad or nervous or doubt themselves. This is a common misconception. Being tough doesn't mean you don't feel any negative emotions. All emotions are part of the human experience, and everyone feels them. By looking at the negative emotion and understanding it, you can move forward.

2. Myth: Either you were born tough, or you were not. This is definitely not true. It is possible to strengthen your mental toughness on purpose. Skills to build this ability are straightforward and will make big, positive changes in your life.

3. Myth: People who aren't tough have a negative attitude. A negative attitude isn't the deciding factor in mental toughness. Strengthening mental toughness also has to do with taking positive action and changing negative behaviors.

4. Myth: Mental toughness only works in sports. This belief is false. Mental toughness skills improve all areas of your life. They improve relationships, enthusiasm, and drive, regardless of the state of your life.

5. Myth: If your mind is tough, you won't have any more problems. Unfortunately, life isn't always perfect or fair. It ebbs and flows, and we cannot always control it. Implementing these skills as habits will help you in times of ease and in times of stress.

The Benefits of Mental Strength Training

When you practice the skills that go into being mentally tough, you'll notice positive changes in your life. Bouncing back from adversity doesn't necessarily mean things will return to normal. It often means you can reach a better place. Consider these benefits:

1. Mental toughness strengthens motivation and drive. Practicing mental toughness skills empowers you to excel. Objectively analyzing a situation will help you take more responsibility for your happiness. This will strengthen your confidence and willingness to take calculated risks.

2. Mentally tough people make good leaders. They know how to empower others. Good leaders know they can't succeed on their own. Strengthening mental toughness will increase your ability to problem-solve and get the help you need from parents, teachers, coaches, or friends.

3. Self-awareness and self-motivation increase when you are mentally tough. Knowing yourself means knowing when you need to take a break. Setting boundaries with parents, coaches, friends, and yourself will get easier as you practice mental toughness skills.

4. Improving mental toughness will build your ability to accept what life throws your way. You understand things will improve. You will worry less about the worst-case scenario or the things you can't control.

In short, mental toughness skills increase your ability to cope with stress, overcome setbacks, solve problems, remain task-focused, perform under pressure, increase your confidence and decrease helplessness, depression, and anxiety.

How to use new skills in practice.

Implementing new habits can be difficult, especially when they involve breaking old habits. You can learn something from everything you encounter, and this is an excellent opportunity to improve your self-worth and enthusiasm for your sport, school, and life. When you learn something new, it's easy to beat yourself up for not getting it correct right away. Learn to avoid self-judgment. If something doesn't work, try again. Make adjustments if you need to. Go easy on yourself when you're discovering what works for you.

Keeping a journal can help you get your thoughts out, so you don't have to keep them in your brain. Sometimes it's overwhelming to have so many thoughts swirling around like a whirlpool. Writing it out can help ease that feeling and gain some distance and perspective on the issue. Set a timer for 10 minutes and write whatever comes to you, even if it makes little sense. *(See resource page for journal suggestions)*

One skill you'll learn emphasizes building a community of support. You can use this skill to implement changes you want to make by asking for accountability and support. Having people around you who know the changes you're trying to make will remind you of your goals and help you stick to them.

As your self-awareness improves, you will maintain a positive outlook on your progress. When you can look back at the work you've done and be proud of yourself despite not being perfect, you'll gain confidence in your ability to grow and excel. Remember, despite what social media depicts, no-one is perfect. In fact, one of the most useful life hacks to raise your feelings of wellbeing is to limit your use of social media. If you are constantly comparing yourself to what you see on social media and feel like you are not enough or don't measure up, it might be time to take a break. Part of mental toughness is facing difficult emotional triggers head-on. Explore how to handle those emotions correctly in the next chapter.

Chapter Three

Skill 2: How to Control Your Emotions

If you're wondering how someone who was a part-time player in her junior year got the attention of recruiters without being a star on the big stage at the big scouting tournament, then you need to finish reading this book.

The reality of college recruiting is that college coaches don't recruit talent or stats, they recruit character. They want you to be a team player and work hard. In college, the game you love becomes a full-time occupation that requires resilience and grit. While you will need a base level of talent to compete, you will need robust character to excel. These principles hold true at every level of competition.

I was fortunate to have the support of my dad to help guide me towards the correct response to the situation I was in. In the build-up to the big scouting tournament, we spoke frequently about my frustration, my concerns, and what to do about it. By this stage in my softball career we had built a sincere, trusting relationship. We could speak openly and candidly. He was the manager for many of my teams. Unlike many dad coaches, he did not automatically pencil me into the starting lineup, but made me earn my starting position.

When I was eight years old, I played on my first travel team. I wanted to be the starting second baseman. I remember being frustrated that I was not getting to play as often as I wanted. Dad provided an explanation. The starting player was better than me. He explained reality to me. I needed to play the game better than the person in front of me. He told me I could force the coach to play me by becoming a better player. He said I needed to work harder at practice than any other player. I needed to work on my defensive footwork and to improve my bat-to-ball skills. The best players got better by outworking their competition. He was confident I could be a starting player, but I had to be ready to perform when I got my opportunity. That is a lesson I never forgot.

Coincidentally, during the state championship tournament at the end of our season, we ended up taking second place. I started the last two games. I got 6 base hits that put our team in a position to win. My coach was so surprised by my performance he asked where I had been all season. As an 8-year-old, I hadn't developed into full smart ass mode yet so I simply answered, "**right here on the bench, coach.**"

Eight years later, as my father and I were traveling to this final big scouting tournament where we knew I would not get much playing time, he reminded me of that story. He provided another simple message: If you will be a role player on this team, then you should be the best role player you can be. Be the hardest worker in practice. Be the loudest cheerleader. Support your teammates with enthusiasm. And when you get your limited opportunities, play hard, have fun and let your character shine.

Many coaches recruiting me had seen me play for the past few years. They knew what I was capable of athletically. I was never the most gifted athlete on any of my teams, but I always helped my teams win. I played with joy and enthusiasm. Sometimes I would get the big hit to drive in key runs and other times I would make a stellar defensive play to save a run. But I always gave my best effort and did what my coaches asked of me.

I hustled on and off the field despite only warming up the pitcher. I was the loudest supporter of my teammates. When I expected an upcoming pinch-hit opportunity, I would get out the batting tee and prepare myself for the big at-bat. And in my 7 opportunities, I hit the ball hard in each at-bat and drove in some runs.

After our last game, my dad gave me a big hug and told me how proud he was of my effort. I loved his support and appreciated it. But I was stunned when several coaches approached me to set up campus visits because they watched and saw how I handled this adversity. They had watched me play in previous years and knew the coach I was playing for was less than reputable. They saw value in how I handled the situation and wanted me on their team.

Everyone competing in those games has athletic talent. But colleges coaches have a limited budget to invest in their players. They don't want to be around athletes that don't fit their program. Coaches want to see how you handle failure or adversity because it will inevitably happen at any level of competition.

As my story shows, there isn't much that we have direct control over in our lives. For example, we cannot control other people, the weather, or traffic. Though it may seem difficult, we **can** control our reactions to the situations we have no control over.

Teenagers routinely feel as if they have no control over their emotions. They have never dealt with hormones, social situations, or dating before. Specific mental toughness skills can improve your ability to walk mindfully through your feelings, productively.

Having the ability to regulate emotions helps you, rather than hurts you. The development of this skill will lead to more mental toughness by providing a way to feel emotions without letting them control your behavior.

The inability to properly regulate emotions leads to negative outcomes. These include inconsistency in performance, lack of confidence, and lack of energy from the stress. Working on emotion regulation will help you identify potential issues with your current responses. It will help you react to situations more productively moving forward. It will help you address what is causing your negative emotion without engulfing you in negativity.

Re-Frame the Situation

There are several ways to regulate your emotions. Cognitive reframing is the ideal way to begin. This involves changing your counterproductive perspective on an event or situation into an effective one.

It's easy to assume that the worst thing possible is going to happen. It's easy to make assumptions. We speculate why coaches make certain decisions. If we do something wrong, what will our teammates think about us? We stress over the weird look we get from someone. We worry about our future. It's easy to wonder what the next unfortunate thing will be.

Focusing on what happened and what might happen in the future causes unnecessary worry and stress. It frequently leads to further negative emotions. It's impossible to mind-read. We cannot tell the future. By attempting to do so, frustration increases, and the negative thoughts spiral downward. Instead, look at the situation objectively to consider other scenarios.

For example, imagine you're hanging out with teammates before practice, and someone gives you a nasty look that communicates anger. Immediately, your mind may race to the things that could be wrong. You may feel hurt and like you have done something offensive.

If you believe your action caused their reaction, you may become anxious or worried. Negative emotions may become heightened. And because of heightened emotions, your thoughts spin out of control. They may influence your behavior. You may say or do something that makes the matter worse.

Making assumptions is risky and not helpful. You should pause and re-reframe your perspective.

Rather than thinking your teammate is mad at you, you could reframe that thought. They might have had a rough day. Perhaps their nasty face had nothing to do with you. They could have been looking behind you.

By thinking of the situation differently, you'll feel your anxiety lessen and your emotions will not turn into something too powerful to handle.

The biggest key to cognitively reframing a situation is to consider, **Is this working for me?** As you notice your emotions getting carried away or your thoughts spiraling, hit the pause button. Ask yourself, **Is this helping?** Give yourself the time and space to slow down and consider alternative explanations for the events you experience. Reframe the situation until your thoughts and emotions are more productive.

Reframing Drill

As you practice and play, pay attention to what you are thinking and feeling and how it's affecting your performance.

Identify a specific event that happened in the past 2 weeks. Select an event from a practice or game where your emotions caused you to act in a way you're not proud of. Then answer the next series of questions about that specific moment.

- What are the specific thoughts you were having? Write them in your journal. Censor nothing. What actual words, interpretations, thoughts went through your head?

- How did these thoughts affect you? What emotions did they lead to? Be as descriptive as possible. Try to name the exact intensity of the emotion you were experiencing.

- What reactions did these emotions cause? Did you throw equipment on the ground or yell at someone? Did it cause a physiological response such as a heart rate spike, tense muscles, eye rolling?

- Were your emotions and reactions in this situation productive? (helpful) Or counterproductive? (not helpful) Why?

- If the situation was counterproductive, reconsider the initial event. What really happened? Did you make assumptions that were incorrect? Is there an alternative explanation for what happened? Can you do something different if it happens again? How can you think more effectively next time something like this happens?

This information creates new options for you. Use it to better take control of your mental process and set conditions for success. The more you practice reframing your thoughts, the better able you will be to make adjustments and enhance your performance in real time.

However, when you feel powerful emotions, you don't always have to push them down and tell them not to exist.

Allow Negative Emotions

It's important to understand that all emotions are valid. If you believe there are certain emotions you're not allowed or shouldn't feel, those emotions won't go away. Instead, they'll make their way into the words you speak and your behavior. This will hinder your ability to regulate emotions in the future.

Practice accepting your emotions, and you'll notice that it's easier to feel them. Acceptance doesn't mean you have to be pleased with your emotions or enjoy them. It doesn't mean you have to be at peace with the current situation. Accepting your emotions simply means acknowledging the truth of what you feel.

The amount of playing time you are currently getting might frustrate you. You don't have to like it. Experiencing frustration can motivate you to make the changes needed to get better.

Rather than trying to ignore your emotions, label them instead. When you can label what you're feeling as an emotion, you'll notice the emotion doesn't feel like it's controlling you as much. Let's say, that right now you are feeling anger. By saying **I am angry** and acknowledging it's affecting you, you'll notice the emotion doesn't feel as big, you might notice your heart rate slowing down and your breath returning to normal.

It isn't easy to acknowledge your emotions and not react to them. One way to develop this skill further is by practicing mindfulness skills.

Mindfulness encourages non-judgmental awareness and will help you sit with your feelings rather than react to them.

Mindfulness Drills

Practice these mindfulness skills for emotion regulation:

- Observe your breathing. Set a timer for three minutes and simply notice your breathing. There is no need to be specific. If you can spend time simply noticing your breath, you'll feel calm. When your mind wanders, just go back to noticing your breath.

- Spend ten minutes coloring. Whether you consider yourself creative or not, coloring in a coloring book is a great way to focus on one thing instead of getting swallowed up by emotions. Pick something to color that is enjoyable to you. Consider grabbing the kids' menu at the next restaurant you go to and remind yourself of a simpler time.

- Ground yourself. Sometimes our thoughts and emotions get stuck in our head and we can't move on. Grounding is a simple technique. **Pick three things you can see, hear, and feel**. For example, in this specific moment of writing, I can see my computer screen, my keyboard, the bangs in my face as I type. I can hear kids playing basketball next door, the sound of my keyboard, and the music I have playing. I can feel the inside of my fuzzy slippers, my bum on my mesh office chair, and a tight muscle on my back from my workout yesterday. Grounding helps **you get out of your head** and into the present.

- Getting outside is a path to mindfulness when you do it with intention. Walk outside with the intention of simply noticing. Observe your surroundings and name the things you see, hear, or smell. You could even consider people watching and trying to imagine their story.

- If you are feeling powerful emotions, visualize your emotions floating by like clouds in the sky. Close your eyes and imagine a beautiful place that is serene and comforting. Next, imagine that cloud gently passing by. Place one of your troubles on that cloud and watch it peacefully pass onward.

Mindfulness helps to tether us to the present moment. These skills build mental toughness and enhance your quality of life. Doing these things daily helps strengthen your brain function and reminds you of good coping skills in the future. It helps you acknowledge your emotions without judgment and gain the pause needed to react in more helpful ways to whatever emotion you are experiencing.

Apps can be a great way to build your mindfulness muscle. They often teach and guide you through mindfulness practices of different lengths, have different topics, and just require you to follow along. *(See the resource page for mindfulness resources)*

Increase Positive Emotions

Whether you're in a time of distress or a time of peace, it's important to have positive experiences. Sometimes we forget to have fun because of the hustle and bustle of life. Set yourself up for success by having a good time doing something you enjoy. Having a store of positive memories and positive emotions helps give hope when times are difficult or things aren't going your way. When you are struggling, try doing something you've previously enjoyed. Give yourself permission to have a delightful time, even if things feel like they're falling apart around you.

You can increase positive emotions by doing things you enjoy. You can watch your favorite stand-up comedian, go on a hike in the woods, go hang out with your friends or enjoy making your favorite recipe. It can be as simple as walking or showering. Just be mindful while doing so. Practicing gratitude brings positivity, even when it's hard to stay positive.

Gratitude Drill

Make a gratitude list or engage in the ***Three Good Things*** activity each day. Experience what happens to your attitude. You don't have to conjure grand things to be grateful for. If you like the pen you write with, be grateful for that pen. It could be something you are looking forward to or a nice thing someone did for you. If you're having a bad day and can't think of anything, practice being grateful for the oxygen you breathe, your pet, or your favorite meal. (See resources page for Three Good Things journal options)

Here's how to do it:

1. Reflect on what you are grateful for as you prepare for bed.

2. Write three things that went well today. Draft a reflection using these questions as prompts (pick the ones that apply). **Why did this happen? What does this mean to you? How could I get more of this? How did you or someone else contribute to the good thing?**

3. Maintain this gratitude journal for at least 1 week. Do your best to not repeat anything you write. Find unique things daily.

There are other ways to build positive emotion. You can change your current outlook by balancing your negative thoughts with some productive thoughts. Fixed mindset athletes think, **I am not capable of doing this**. Growth mindset athletes think, **I have not learned this yet**. This offers a shift in perspective that will help you tolerate emotional distress. Fixed mindset people artificially limit themselves. Growth mindset people never stop learning and improving.

Regulating your emotions is a powerful tool for mental toughness. This skill allows you to sit with emotions and move on from them without making impulsive decisions or letting them control your body. Life is stressful. It can feel like you are spinning out of control sometimes. However, you can prevent your reaction from causing a cascade of negative effects by using the tools above.

Personal Story

In my sophomore year of high school, my school softball team was playing for the championship in our division (you heard a bit about this in the introduction). We were the visiting team, so we were batting first. I was the cleanup batter. In my first at-bat, there were bases loaded and no outs. My heart was racing as I walked to the plate. I was worried about the outcome rather than the process. I knew I needed to calm down, but even though I was trying to take nice big breaths, I just couldn't slow down my heart rate.

Up to this point, I had played many big games before on my travel team. I have had games come down to my at-bat, but for whatever reason, this game, this at bat, I was not calm or collected, and the tricks I normally used weren't working. By objective terms, I had a decent at bat. I went deep in the count and fouled off several pitches, but I could tell my swing was not smooth. I took the last pitch without swinging because I was stuck in my head. Now, to this day, I truly believe that pitch was not actually a strike. But I should never have given the umpire the opportunity to affect my at bat. The pitcher was not overpowering. I had gotten several good pitches to hit in that at bat. I just couldn't connect because of how nervous I was. We ended up losing that game by one run. I could have changed the outcome of the game. But I'd been unable to perform at my best (or even just my normal capacity) because I let my nerves get to me.

I was making the moment bigger than it was. I interpreted the situation as **I have to get a hit. The game depends on this at bat! All my friends from school are here watching.** I wanted to be the hero. And because I was overthinking this, my nerves were on edge. I couldn't control my heart rate and that affected everything else from there. I might have been more successful if I had used the reframing drill or emotion regulation skills. I should have known that it was okay to be nervous. I should have channeled the nervous excitement to perform better and help the team. Instead of thinking the entire game was resting on me, I should have been able to keep my physiology under control. By framing the situation correctly, I would have had a better chance of succeeding.

Chapter Four

Skill 3: How to Improve Consistency

As a teenager, you can't control much. Understanding and accepting that fact will provide freedom from a lot of unnecessary stress and worry. You may not have the power to control what is happening. However, you always have the power to control how you respond to what happens.

By managing the power to control our reactions to situations, we also have the power to control the next action we take. Be objective and evaluate the situation to get accurate information about any issue. It takes humility to see what you could have done differently. Every situation gives you the chance to learn about yourself. It is possible to understand without judgment and with compassion to make wise, well-informed decisions. This will help you grow and develop as an athlete and a person.

Get Curious

Taking responsibility for your part of any situation can help you take charge of your life. You can realize your power to overcome when you look at your life and role without bias. Begin by getting curious about the situation. For example, if your coach barks at you, you might ask, **Was there anything I could have done differently? Or what can I learn from this to help me in the next (play, match, game, drill)?**

Remember to have a non-judgmental attitude. If you're criticizing yourself, you're not taking responsibility but digging yourself further into the challenge at the risk of destroying your confidence. You shouldn't think everything is your fault, especially when things go wrong. This is a common error in logic that influences many mental health issues. Most of the time, it isn't. Problems are rarely 100% your fault or 100% someone else's fault. Most often, the truth is somewhere in the middle. However, it will strengthen your mental toughness to take an honest look at your part in your circumstance.

As a team sport athlete, making a costly error or mistake does not mean you were the sole cause of a loss. You influenced the loss, but you aren't the only one on the team. You weren't the only one out there playing. As an individual sport athlete, even though you are the only one competing, losses still aren't 100% under your control. There are still other athletes you are competing against, and their performance influences your success. You can do everything right, perform your absolute best, and still lose. That is the nature of competition.

Sometimes taking ownership of your actions can be difficult. It's important to have humility, especially if you need to apologize to others. Your ability to verbalize your wrongdoings, errors, or mistakes will display your maturity and ability to regulate your emotions. This is an integral part of being a coachable student-athlete. If you cannot take reasonable accountability for your own actions, work ethic, or thought process, it is almost impossible to coach you. If you always blame others for your failures, you will never improve. You will only get better if you're open to feedback.

Get Curious Drill

1. Think about a recent failure you have experienced. Then use the next few steps to get curious about the situation.

2. Slow down: take a moment to tune into your thoughts and assess where you are placing the blame for your current situation. Is it all your fault? Are you blaming everything and everyone else? Are you doing a bit of both?

3. Ask critical questions: Regardless of who or what you blamed for a failure moment, make sure you accurately assess what happened. How did you contribute to this situation? How much was someone else responsible? Gaining better accuracy about what is and isn't your fault allows you to move forward with purpose.

4. Make a Plan: Develop a plan to improve the factors that you influenced. Then practice accepting the factors that you could not control (weather, field conditions, umpires, refs, other players).

As you practice, the get curious drill for situations that have already happened, an interesting thing will occur. It will be easier for you to use the skill when you experience a failure in real time. In those cases, consider the following plan;

1. **Slow down**

2. **Ask critical questions**

3. **Develop a plan to** become your process for being coachable in any moment.

If you are struggling with the process, involve an objective third party (like a parent or coach) to help you get more accurate or build a plan to improve.

Making Changes

It's difficult to understand how to take responsibility for your own happiness and mental toughness. When things feel out of control and chaotic, it can seem even harder. However, you can learn to implement changes that last.

Begin by implementing consistent routines. Perform the same routine each morning, before a competition, or test, to help you get prepared to succeed. Include a few minutes for a mindfulness exercise (consider breathing or grounding from the previous chapter, right before performance moments).

You can schedule your time to help you set boundaries and keep track of your personal growth. You should keep track of your school schedule (tests, major assignments, etc) and your sports schedule (games, practices, travel, etc).

This gives you the information you need to decide about prioritizing your time. Sometimes sports need to take a back seat to other priorities. Or your primary sport might need to take priority over your secondary sport or vice versa. There will always be major commitments competing for your time. You can pre-plan how to manage those moments. This helps reduce the stress that these decisions can cause.

If you are prone to worry, use your phone to set consistency drill reminders throughout the day. The reminders can help you pause in the present moment, do the drill and move forward. Maybe you're in the middle of a crisis and a reminder goes off. This will remind you that you get to make your own decision.

You should check-in with yourself a few times a day to gauge your mental status. By building the practice of identifying your thoughts, emotions, and physiology, you'll be better able to take responsibility for them and make changes that meet your needs. When you identify your thoughts, emotions and physiology in low stress moments, you'll be better able to identify them in bigger, more pressure-filled moments which will enable greater self-control and the ability to be clutch in those moments.

See every moment as a learning opportunity. Ask yourself, **What am I learning from this?** Thinking about this will help you feel more empowered to change your habits, because it will increase curiosity and self-confidence.

Consistency Drill

1. You can set an alarm on your phone to go off three different times. One in the morning, around lunch and evening.

2. Every time the alarm/reminder goes off, pause and do a short self-reflection. Ask yourself what you are thinking, feeling, and what you notice in your body.

3. Then ask, **is this working for me?** Are your thoughts, emotions, and feelings helping you to be effective in the moment? Or are they counterproductive and getting in your way?

4. If they are working for you, great, carry on. Keep doing your thing. If they aren't working, use the drills in the book to change your thinking. You'll be able to build mental toughness if you work at it.

Personal Story

The story of my failure during the championship game in my sophomore year continued to affect me even into the next season. Because I went to a small school, only one other teammate played travel ball. Because I had higher expectations of myself than my teammates, I took on the responsibility of losing the championship game during the next school softball season. I internalized we would have won the game if I had gotten a hit at that point. Yet, other players had opportunities to get hits in the first inning. And there were 6 more innings in the game. But I felt the loss was my responsibility.

Then my Junior season began. I felt I needed to be perfect if we were going to win. Then I began pressing, and I lost my aggressive, confident attitude because I was worried about making mistakes. Finally, I struggled against pitchers that I normally dominated. They should not have been a problem.

My dad noticed this shift (about 2 weeks later) and contracted with a sport psychologist to work through these issues for me. What the psychologist helped me figure out (through critical questions and curiosity) was, yes I played a role in our team's loss, but it was not **all** my fault. We worked through breathing exercises and mindfulness practices (singing a favorite song) to better control my body (heart rate) in big moments. He helped me change the flawed thinking that was preventing me from playing at my best. I learned to have more realistic and productive expectations of myself. I let go of the pressure I was putting on myself.

Most of the players from that losing team returned for my junior season. We were hungry and angry about the way we lost the previous season. We ended up making the playoffs and returning to the championship game. Because of the skills my sports psychologist taught me, I was better able to control my emotions, expectations, and enjoyment of the games. In fact, throughout the playoffs, I had a lot of success. My sports psychology training kicked in with a vengeance during the playoffs. I got the game-winning hit in every game leading up to the championship.

Once again, we reached the State Championship game. In the clutch moment, I stayed confident, calm, and performed. As you already know from the introduction, I drove in the winning run during the bottom of the tenth inning. My team got a walk-off win for the ages! Go Lions! The entire school was there, and it was one of my favorite softball moments in my life. I got to run and tackle my teammates as we laughed, cried, and cheered our victory.

By learning to accept my true role in the previous year's loss, to acknowledge that it was a team effort, and how to manage the mistakes I made the previous year, I was even more successful the next year.

Chapter Five

Skill 4: How to Build Your Champion Support Team

Increasing mental toughness means building a strong support community. As human beings, we need to feel a sense of belonging. We are social creatures not meant to live alone. We strive to be a part of something bigger than ourselves. According to Abraham Maslow's hierarchy of needs, once a person satisfies their physiologic and safety needs, they strive to be loved and belong in a community. Once meeting these needs, a person will seek high self-esteem and self-actualization. It will be difficult to excel at your sport without a support framework. You need to build a community that supports your goals and aligns with your ambition if you want to reach the highest level of your sport. I call this community your Champion Support Team.

You don't need to have many people on your team, but research shows that as a teenager, having at least one trusted adult in your life is vital to your resilience and mental toughness. It's also important to reach out and make new connections when needed.

A champion support team is a powerful catalyst for a meaningful life. Having others to share our highs and lows with gives a stronger sense of purpose and acceptance. When we're going through difficult times, it's of the utmost importance to hold on to your champion support team. This can be family, friends, a team, or a hobby group.

Other people can serve as guideposts, cheerleaders, and supporters when we let them in. Building a support team can make you feel vulnerable because you have to reveal your flaws. The sooner you learn to embrace your failures as keys to growth, the better off you will be.

It's also important to choose the right support team. You become who you surround yourself with. It would be a wise practice to surround yourself with people with similar goals and drive. It can destroy your success if people with different priorities surrounded you. They will drag you away from your goals, eventually.

Willpower can only last so long. Let's assume your goal is to finish all your homework and get good grades in school, so that you can be eligible to play your sport. If your social group doesn't care about school, they may interrupt you during study hall or give you crap for doing your work instead of just hanging out. Your willpower will wane and you'll tire of telling them you need to study and start hanging out. This could be disastrous if your grades suffer.

College coaches investing a four-year scholarship offer want to make sure the student athlete can graduate. Your ability to earn good grades gives coaches confidence you can handle college coursework. Surround yourself with people who will support your goals. It might feel scary at first, and then it will feel freeing.

Build Your Champion Support Team Drills

Try these techniques to build your support team:

1. Analyze your current community. Look at the people around you and examine your relationships with them. Do you need stronger relationships within your support team? Do you need more people on your team to support you in different ways? Can you communicate effectively with your support team when necessary? Do you need to remove people from your team?

2. Strengthen connections. Bonding with friends is important, and you can do so by inviting your friends to take part in activities you're interested in. Doing things you enjoy doing with people you care about strengthens your relationships.

3. Allow time for conversation. Actively listen to your friends by responding to what they have to say and staying off your phone. I know this is tough, but **it really matters**. Through conversation, you will allow your friends to get to know you better.

4. Join a group. There are plenty of people interested in things you love. You can benefit from a group of people when you engage with them. It is possible to do this online but do some research. Make sure the group works for you.

5. Be generous to others. In order to attract quality friends, you need to be worthy of their friendship. Don't be the person who always takes but never gives. One-sided relationships don't last. Be helpful to others and you will discover how quickly you can attract friends.

6. Show Gratitude. You can build quality relationships with your team by letting them know how much they mean to you. It's difficult to find good friends, and expressing gratitude is a great way to make friends. Practice saying "thank you" to people on your Champion Support Team such as parents, coaches, teachers. Remember, they are not your servant they are a willing partner on your team. If a parent rushes home from work and eats dinner in the car in order to take you to practice, offer a **Thank You**.

Most of your coaches are volunteers who give up hours of their lives to make your sport possible. Thank people for their time and effort. It makes your athletic dream possible. If your friend helps you do chores around the house so that you can go hangout, say Thank You. Let people know you appreciate what they do for you. This is an effective way to show appreciation and to build stronger bonds.

7. **Be authentic**. Authenticity breeds inner peace and stronger relationships. Become self-aware of how you appear to others. Are you playing a role or are you acting like the real you? Pay attention to how you feel. When you act in a certain way, does it feel true to you? Do you feel energized by acting that way? Are you internally motivated to do that action? If so, you are being authentic. If you feel like a fake, like you are trying to be someone you are not, or if you have to be pressured into acting like you care, then you are not being authentic. That creates inner turmoil and mental fatigue. It's not authentic to who you are at your core. You don't have just one identity. You aren't just an athlete, you have other interests, passions, hobbies, etc. Do your best to be authentic to your whole self, not just to individual parts of you.

Communicate

Communication is essential to daily life. Working on communication skills will enhance the connections you have with others and help you build new bridges. Excellent communication begins with intentional listening. Nothing will get done if someone isn't good at listening. Actively listen to those you're engaging with. You can do this by making eye contact with them, facing them, and listening to what they're saying. Good listeners let people finish what they are saying without interruption. They can repeat back what they heard. If your mind is wandering, that means you're drifting from the present moment. Bring your attention back to your conversation.

Body language has a significant impact on communication. Some estimates say that 55% of all communication is based on body language. Relieve the tension in your body. Relax your arms and shoulders, and don't cross your arms. This simple posture frequently blocks effective communication. Crossed arms communicate you are unwilling to engage with someone. Closed-off body language sets a negative tone. Open and positive body language is better for conversations and coaching sessions. Don't let your body language poison your relationship with your coach. Doing your best to show that you are listening, goes a long way to helping your coach understand you want to learn and get better.

Show confidence when speaking to others. If you lack the confidence to start conversations with adults or strangers, that's okay. It becomes something you must learn to do. Practice is the way to get better. You can increase confidence by standing tall and being aware of what you say. Speak and listen with intent. Having confident body language will help you become more confident.

During competitive sporting events, your body language gives your opponents clues to your confidence, focus, and ability to compete. Your body language can either intimidate or embolden your opponent. Tough-minded athletes know how to use body language to communicate confidence. And they also know how to read their opponent's body language for clues to their confidence.

Communication Drills

1. Listening Drill - Practice this with a parent or friend. Make sure they know what you are doing, otherwise it could be awkward. Ask your parent or friend to tell you something about their day or an upcoming event. Your task is to listen only! Listen without trying to interrupt or interject. This is a mindfulness practice and a connection opportunity. As you listen, keep your mind focused on the speaker and pay attention to what they are sharing.

2. Coaching Drill – The next time you are receiving feedback/instruction from a coach, pay attention to your body language. Are you making eye contact? Is your body reacting? (muscle tension, heart rate) Has your posture changed? (head shoulders slumped, head up and listening) What are you thinking about? Are you listening or are you planning a response? Are you paying attention with a growth mindset that **feedback is helpful,** even if the feedback is uncomfortable to hear? The goal is to be present so that you can grow from the experience. If you find your mind wandering, focus on taking a deep breath, shifting your posture, and trying not to make excuses.

3. Communication Drill – If you need to have an uncomfortable

conversation, take some time to plan what you want to say. Clarifying what you want to say and how you want to say it can be difficult. Clarify the actual issue you want to bring up. How can you describe it without exaggeration? How can you express your concerns or emotions about the issue in a way that doesn't attack the other person? Say things like **when (blank) happened, it made me feel (blank)** instead of **you made me mad**. Taking the time to plan out what you want to say helps you feel more confident. It will also help you be concise and to the point.

Remain Accountable

A champion support team is a group of people who support you during rough times. When you're down, they will help lift you up. When you're celebrating, they will celebrate with you.

These kinds of connections add a stronger sense of purpose and meaning in life. If you're hoping to implement some changes in your daily routine, you can call on people on your support team to hold you accountable. Let your friends know what you want to accomplish and what your timeline is.

For example, if you're hoping to finish an assignment by Wednesday, so you don't have to do it after your game on Thursday, let some of your friends know your goal. Once Wednesday rolls around, they can ask you whether you finished your assignment. If you're nervous to talk to your coach about something, you can ask one of your teammates to join you to ease the stress that being alone can bring.

Having a strong champion support team builds mental toughness by ensuring you have people who have your back.

If you're going through a difficult time, you can rely on your support team to provide encouragement and guidance. If you're stuck in a rut and don't know what to do next, you can consult your support team. They can offer new perspectives and give you ideas for solutions you had not thought of.

You never have to worry about being a burden on your support team. They can offer light in times of darkness, and you can do the same for them when they're struggling.

A place where you feel accepted is the purpose of a community and champion support team. By feeling accepted, you'll find a stronger feeling of hope. Others can help bring you back to reality when you have tunnel vision during a difficult situation.

Personal Story

One of the significant advantages of playing sports is that you get a built-in community of teammates. During the season, you are all working together for a common purpose (or at least they should be). Finding community for me in high school was a mixed bag. Throughout high school, I was part of some amazing groups of girls (school teams and travel teams) that helped me feel connected. I felt like I belonged. I also had some challenges. Because I was an elite athlete who wanted to play in college, I spent a lot of weekends and most of my summer traveling and playing softball.

This made it tough to maintain school friendships because I missed a lot of birthday parties, dances, other school events, summer outings, and shenanigans. They didn't invite me to hang out in the summer because they thought I was busy. They never called me unless I called them first. That was not fun. While I had good friends on my travel teams, we couldn't hang out outside of softball because we didn't live near each other.

My high school was small. There was a lot of drama. For me, this played out in interesting ways. I played varsity sports all 4 years of high school. During my freshman year, I spent a lot of time with upperclassmen, which made the people in my grade angry. And then, by the time all my classmates were playing varsity, most of my close friends had graduated. I had to rebuild friendships with my grade.

Because I was a tomboy and also the water girl for the football team (my older brother was a captain of the team), most of my best friends in high school were guys. This alienated me from the girls in my class. And then my two best guy friends ditched me. They realized they were spending all their time hanging out with me, and it was hindering their dating life.

Of course, I didn't know this. I didn't learn this until 15 years later, when I had dinner and drinks with the knuckleheads. All I knew at the time was my friends ditched me. And if they had communicated their issues to me, they could have gotten a lot more dates. These stupid boys didn't realize all the girls came to me to ask about them. I knew who liked them, so I could have hooked them up. Plus, it wouldn't have caused me pain with no clue what was happening.

I was fortunate to have some pretty amazing adults as part of my support team. My parents were great. Our relationship wasn't perfect (because… teenager) but they always had my best interests in mind. I had an amazing softball coach at school, Raf. (Scott Raftery) He kept me sane and helped me find the fun in the sport again. He was a giant teddy bear, Disney loving, prankster, goofball, who didn't know how NOT to have fun. His door was always open. He allowed me to share life's burdens with him. And he even had a big ugly green chair for me to sit in.

Once I got to college, my community solidified. And as an adult, I have an amazing set of friends, family, and sense of purpose. But this won't happen for you overnight. You are still figuring out your values and what matters most to you. Friendships will come and go, especially in high school. If you aren't happy with your existing championship support team, find another community. Find a group or multiple groups that give you what you need to help build your champion support team.

If you are nerdy, be a nerd. Artistic types should embrace their art. Scholar types should embrace their studies. It is outstanding if you enjoy everything like I did. Just know that you won't get all your community needs from one set of people. I had my travel softball friends who understood my drive, passion and ambition. I had various high school friends for my daily interactions and connection and my family for unconditional support and love. Look for healthy and supportive communities that can be part of your champion support team.

Chapter Six

Skill 5: How to Build Your Inner Strength

All too often, we ignore and criticize ourselves when what we need most, is self-compassion. Self-compassion involves having an accepting and non-judgmental attitude toward ourselves, no matter what. Part of building mental toughness is building your ability to care for yourself.

Self-Care Basics

The basics are the first step in creating a self-compassionate outlook. It may seem small, but doing intentional things to take care of yourself can alter the way you see yourself.

It may seem silly, but start with hygiene. This is where you can make the quickest adjustments and begin feelings of success. Ensure you brush your teeth each day, for example. Your dentist will be happy, but even more happens. You can spend your time brushing your teeth by thinking of it as a dedicated time where you're taking care of yourself.

When you take a shower, be mindful and notice how the shampoo smells, how clean you feel, and how nice the water feels. Being mindful in this way will increase your ability to care for yourself.

A significant step to building small successes is to make your bed each day. You can start the day with success. Small wins add up. The best way to succeed in the long run is to build a pattern of small successes along the way.

If you're having an off morning and make your bed anyway, you're showing a commitment to yourself and your life. Mental toughness is doing something that you don't feel like doing because you made a commitment to do it. If you can start with making your bed, then you build the capacity to do other things like your homework or training for your sport later.

Pay attention to the food you eat. What we eat affects our brains and bodies, so it's important to nourish your brain and body with nutritious food. You don't have to change your whole diet - you can simply add a few vegetables to your dinner or eat fruit throughout the day. Maybe eat something else besides soda, pizza, and candy. I was a teenager once too, I get it but it's about nutrition and fueling your body.

If you know what your body needs, you can give it to yourself. For example, if you don't like to eat first thing in the morning, pack some decent snacks or some type of portable breakfast. (smoothie, protein bar) Take it to school with you to eat before class once you are fully awake. If you have a practice after school and you lose energy in the afternoon, figure out a way to get some food in you before the practice. If you have an all day tournament, figure out the best way to fuel throughout the day and bring a packed cooler. This is a great path to self-care and better performance. It's tough to make it through a long day of competition if you aren't eating things that fuel your body.

Another self-care idea is to schedule a time each day, or once per week, to care for your surroundings. For example, tidy up your room. Clean the floor, put away clothes, tidy your desk, or do laundry (you're going to need your practice clothes and uniforms). If you can keep up with small tidying times, you'll find that your living space feels lighter and happier. A cluttered space leads to a disorganized mind.

It's important to have the environment you live in reflect your needs and who you are.

If you've decided a tidy room is what you need, and it gets hard to get the motivation to clean your room, ask someone in your support team to help you get started or talk to a friend on the phone while you do it. Often, having someone with us when we need to do boring tasks helps us get the job done, even if they aren't providing practical help.

It can make a difference if you know you have support.

Addressing Critical Self-Talk

How do you talk to yourself? Spend a few days noticing what you say. Start by simply observing the phrases you tell yourself. (Consider using a journal to keep track of what you think and feel.)

What do you think when you have a success? Are you proud of yourself? What do you think about after making a mistake? Do you beat yourself up?

Some people have critical self-talk, regardless of their success. If they play well, they might think, I have to be perfect, or I could have done better. And when they make a mistake, the critical talk gets even worse. They might think, I am worthless, or I did nothing right.

A common misconception is that critical self-talk is a wonderful motivator. But it rarely is, especially as a teenager who is still trying to build their confidence and self-esteem.

Saying, **I'm outstanding, I got this, I'm good at blank, or I am worthy,** to yourself is not something to be embarrassed about. It may seem conceited at first. However, positive self-talk isn't conceited because it's in your head and no one else can hear it. Productive self-talk is essential to build confidence, self-worth, and motivation. Our thoughts drive our emotions and how we behave in the world, so it's important to ensure that the thinking you engage in leads to effective emotions and actions.

Negative self-talk frequently takes an athlete out of the performance zone they need to play their best. If you thrive off critical commentary, try changing your thoughts to self-compassionate ones and seeing what happens.

It may appear difficult to change your thoughts. Thankfully, it's not when you willingly commit to do so. The more you practice, the easier it becomes.

Your self-talk should follow some basic principles. It should be purposeful, which means you are thinking it intentionally and deliberately. You are not leaving your thoughts up to chance; they aren't random. By filling your head with purposeful thoughts, you don't leave space for the random ineffective thoughts to come in.

It will be productive, if your self talk helps you stay focused, confident or motivated. If it doesn't lead to any of those 3 outcomes, it's ineffective. No matter the actual words you use in your head, the goal should be focus, confidence, or motivation.

You should also focus your thoughts on what's possible instead of putting limits on yourself. They should sound more like **I can**, vs **I can't**. For example, if your thoughts are, **I will never reach this goal. I can't do this**. You can turn that phrase around. Instead, say, **I am a hard worker capable of reaching my goals**, or **it may take some time, but I'll get there.**

After you uncover the negative things you say to yourself, balance those things out with thoughts that fit the purposeful, productive and possibility criteria instead. Use the drills below to help you retrain your self-talk.

Critical Self-Talk Drills

1. I Can't Drill: If you're struggling to achieve something and your thoughts have turned unhelpful, then try adding the word **yet**, to the end of the thought. For example, if you are struggling to learn a specific technique in your sport and you have problems during the drills, you might think, **I'm just not good at this**, or **I can't do this**. If you put a **yet** to the end of the thought, **I'm not good at this yet** or **I can't do this yet**, it changes the dynamics of the statement. This **YET** acknowledges the reality of your current skill level but also allows you to remember that you can and will get better if you keep putting in the work. It keeps your thoughts focused on what's possible, even if your current state is not where you want to be. This is also a good time to ask for help from someone who can provide encouragement or instruction to get where you want to be.

2. Best Friend Drill: Another way to change your self-talk to be more effective is to ask, **Would you say that to your best friend?** If you were talking to your best friend the same way you are talking to yourself, would they still be your friend? To change your thinking, ask yourself, what would I say to my best friend if they were dealing with the same thing? How would I help them? And then fill your brain with those thoughts instead of the negative ones you were having.

3. Self-Praise Drill: When you've had a long day of hard work/training, you can look in the mirror and say **you worked hard today. Great job.** Talking to yourself in the mirror may seem strange or uncomfortable, but it is often helpful. Try saying nice things to yourself in the mirror once a day for a continuous period (start with one week) and pay attention to any changes you experience in your thinking. You'll notice that your self-talk gets nicer and more productive throughout the rest of your day, and you are kinder to yourself.

Take Time to Care

It's important to take hold of our thoughts when we're noticing critical self-talk. Thoughts are simply words, they are not facts. You can watch them float by, you can replace them with positive affirmations, and you can ask for help to get over them.

Taking action to love yourself is just as important as changing the way you talk to yourself. You can do this in small ways. These self-care routines go above the basics and encourage you to get a bit more creative with doing things that will nourish you.

Self-Compassion Drills:

1. Write yourself a friendly note. It doesn't have to be long. Start with just two sentences. Write something encouraging, like, I am glad you exist, and I am proud of the work you do. You can give yourself the words that will help you feel more confident.

2. Spend an hour outside. Get some fresh air and mindfulness while you spend time at a local park, in the forest, or at the beach. Being in the open air can offer a new sense of calm.

3. Turn off your phone and pay attention to yourself. Take a break from social media, texts, and other notifications that take you out of the present moment. By truly immersing yourself in your own time, you'll build a stronger connection to yourself. If this time feels uncomfortable, use it to say productive things to yourself.

4. Write it out. Keep a journal or notebook for positive, encouraging thoughts about yourself. Write out some critical self-talk phrases and then come up with counter or balancing thoughts that work for you. *(see resource section for journal options)*

Take the time to take care of yourself. By strengthening the relationship you have with yourself, you'll see other parts of your life improve too. Your relationships will be more authentic, you'll feel more motivated, and mistakes will not make you feel like a total failure.

These habits will improve mental toughness by helping you self-motivate, feel more confident and focus when things are difficult. By practicing self-compassion and effective thinking, you're strengthening yourself to handle everything sport or life throws your way. If you can face difficulty without berating yourself, you'll stand tall and remain hopeful.

Personal Story

For me, self-care in high school came from having clear priorities. I made sure I had time to train for and play softball. I had a calendar that kept track of all my games, travel, and homework/tests. Staying organized helped me prioritize my time and attention. I didn't have to deal with social media and smartphones because they didn't exist when I was in high school, but I had to be diligent about how much I watched TV. I had to negotiate with my parents about keeping my room clean. (my poor mom is one of those people that needs a clean space, I was not.) And this led to some contention. To this day, I only clean my house heavily when Mom is getting ready to visit. But don't tell her that. What she doesn't know won't hurt her.

In my free time, I wanted to chill out, not clean. My parents made a compromise with me. As long as I kept my door closed and brought my laundry down, they would not nag me about my room. I still had to clean it occasionally, especially when we were having company, but for me having one less thing to worry about and getting to keep my room how I wanted it was helpful.

I also spent a lot of my free time reading books. I loved to decompress. Another form of self-care was having clear rules with my parents about the **important** things. Because I played HS sports and travel softball, we figured out what would take precedent over what. There were times, for instance, that I didn't go to high school football games, even though I was a water girl because I had a softball tournament. Sometimes I missed travel ball practice because I had a school volleyball or softball game. I figured out which experiences from school I refused to miss for travel softball (like homecoming, prom and graduation). Making these decisions upfront and being coordinated with my parents helped minimize the amount of mental and emotional energy I spent.

As far as critical self-talk goes, I was fortunate that I didn't have any global issues with this. I was a confident young lady who was successful and knew it. My negative self-talk came in specific situations related to my sport or relationships. And in those cases, I had to reframe the situation and be kind to myself. You heard already how I managed my self-talk for softball situations, so I won't rehash it, but I had to use this tool a lot in my relationships. The situation I mentioned earlier when my two best friends ditched me and stopped hanging out with me outside of school was a tough time. I didn't know why things had changed so suddenly. I had to remind myself constantly that I was a good friend, and that I did nothing wrong. Eventually, I redirected my energy to other relationships, and my negative self-talk subsided. But it was tough for a while. Remembering that tough times don't last forever was a big help.

Chapter Seven

Skill 6: How to Exercise Your Way to Mental Toughness

Exercise increases mental as well as physical toughness. Rigorous exercise trains your body and improves your mood. Athletes get more exercise than the typical teenager. Athletes perform better in all aspects of life than couch potatoes.

Benefits of Exercise

Exercise affects your body and mind. It helps with weight management, muscular health, and muscle memory. Physical activity reduces risk of heart attack, high blood pressure, and premature aging. It also produces biochemical changes in your brain that improve your mental health by decreasing anxiety and improving your sense of wellbeing. Student-athletes often train for the sake of competing. They can lose the joy of exercise. They may have negative associations with certain movements, because coaches used it as a punishment for mistakes. (running laps for being late to practice) or because they don't have a natural affinity for the activity. To help keep yourself motivated to engage in tough physical training, understand and appreciate the benefits exercise has on your mental toughness.

Consider these benefits of exercise

1. Exercise is a natural antidepressant. It relieves depression and improves energy. Exercise produces endorphins that make you feel good. Even If you have no issue with depression, endorphins decrease your risk of becoming depressed. Depression is prevalent among teenagers, but teens who are physically active suffer lower rates of depression.

2. Exercise eases anxiety. It naturally calms the brain and builds new, positive neural pathways. Be mindful while you train for your sport. How does your body feel? When can you relax? What are the sounds you hear? By paying attention to the details of the moment, you're benefiting from mindfulness and easing anxiety.

3. Exercise builds mental toughness by reducing stress. Life can be chaotic and out of control. Exercising can be the one time during your day that you are in control. Exercising consistently reduces overall stress and helps you handle stressful situations more effectively.

4. Exercise releases pent-up energy. Moving your body and appreciating those movements releases negative emotions and encourages positive ones. During exercise, you can temporarily stop focusing on your struggles.

5. Exercise helps you cope. You can feel proud of what your body can do. You can feel proud of your hard work and progress. Giving yourself that positive attention will help you build a comfortable relationship with yourself. Remember, persistent minor victories add up to long-term success.

6. Exercise increases confidence and self-worth. It produces biochemical and neurological changes in your brain. Your brain animates all your movements and controls all of your thoughts.

Exercises improve your brain and your body. The ability to push through a tough workout, gain strength, or master a skill for your sport goes a long way to helping you build competence and confidence. So get your body moving.

Ways to Build Positive Emotion About Exercise

Successful athletes strengthen positive emotions with exercise. Weight lifting, conditioning sessions, lessons, practice, and competitions are sport related. But there are other forms of exercise that improve your wellbeing and mental toughness skills outside of your sport related movements. If you have the time, consider the ideas below to help you feel the joy of exercise for its own sake.

Try These Options

1. Think about outdoor activities other than training for your sport. A walk is a great way to get exercise and engage in mindfulness. You can also go on a hike, surf, snowboard, or take part in your favorite outdoor activity. On a windy day, you could fly a kite. You could go bowling. Just do something active that is not your primary sport.

2. Try something you've never tried before. A fun activity can be an excellent way to get exercise. Plus, it allows you to move without worrying about performance. Try rock climbing, surfing, dancing, yoga, disc golf, pickleball, or whatever interests you. Keep moving and having fun as you move. It will keep you active and improve coordination and balance by working additional muscle groups your primary sport doesn't emphasize.

3. Exercise in your own home. Jump on a trampoline for 15 minutes in the morning to get a great start on your day. Take a dance break while doing homework, listening to your favorite music, and dancing with lightheartedness and fun. Increase the fun aspect when you can get friends, family, or pets to join in. I find dogs provide a natural sense of joy. They love just being able to

run and play.

4. Exercise indoors. Sometimes, it's too hot or cold to do an activity that requires being outside for too long. During inclement weather, swim at an indoor pool, take a yoga class, or find a gym with pickup games and play some random sport you've never tried.

How to Stay Committed with Exercise

Set goals that will help you achieve success as you get started and beyond. Your fitness goals can relate to your sport, or they can relate to your health and mental well-being. You need time away from your sport from time to time. Having a non-sport-related exercise goal can keep you in shape and give your body a break from the repetitive movements of your sport. Use your support system to achieve your goals by asking them to hold you accountable. You can also ask one of your friends to begin an exercise activity with you. If you're helping each other achieve goals, you'll get more excited to move forward. Exercise is an opportunity to satisfy your curiosity about what your body can do.

It's important to let go of perfectionism. Most people don't stand up on the surfboard the first time they surf. That's no reason to give up. When you stick with it and see your progress, you're building the mental toughness that will help you in all areas of your life. You'll notice that the one hour you spend exercising will permeate through your day in larger ways that make you feel calmer and better able to handle outside stressors.

Personal Story

I deliberately played another sport to engage in an exercise that was not my best sport, softball. I went to a small private high school. Because I was a talented athlete, I had the luxury of playing any sport I wanted to. Before high school, I had been playing softball exclusively for about 6 years. And as much as I loved it, I was so excited to try other things! I made the varsity volleyball and soccer teams as a freshman. In California, they were the fall and winter sports, with softball being played in the spring.

I fell in love with volleyball and experienced the challenge of being a newbie and having to earn a starting position. There were no expectations of me playing volleyball other than having some fun. I wasn't worried about impressing coaches or getting recruited. I played carefree. In addition, I played soccer for 1 year. I had a great time and actually ended up building my footwork and speed. But I decided not to play 3 High School sports on top of my travel softball commitments. I overdid it by playing three sports my freshman year and was exhausted by year end. You need to learn the limits of your physical endurance and build recovery time in to your regimen as well. Don't risk injury or exhaustion by doing too much too often. Remember the previous lesson on self care. I learned an important lesson about not spreading myself too thin. But it was still fun.

In college, I couldn't just join multiple teams or even play intramural sports, as softball was a full-time job. But I realized how much playing something other than softball helped me stay balanced. I took PE classes throughout my time in college. This allowed me to sample all kinds of things I would have never tried otherwise (karate, cricket, swimming, ballroom dancing). Some of these have become lifelong pursuits.

Once I was out in the world working, I started taking ballroom dancing lessons for a time (still love it to this day) and ended up getting my 2nd-degree black belt in TaeKwonDo. So imagine a ballroom dancer who can also kick your butt. (Joking) In 2012, I started doing Crossfit. I was having a hard time working out on my own because I missed having teammates (community) around me, and I hated having to decide what to do at the gym. And Crossfit filled those needs for me.

I say all this to highlight that because you are trying to excel in a certain sport doesn't mean you need to spend all your time doing that sport. In fact, for your own sanity and long-term motivation, I would discourage only playing one sport. Let your body experience alternate movements. Let your brain take a break from trying to be the best. Go find an exercise or movement that you enjoy doing for its own sake.

Chapter Eight
Skill 7: How to Set Goals the Right Way

It requires effort to make positive changes. If you want your outcomes (confidence, motivation, focus, energy, better performance) to improve, you will need to take positive action. You can't just keep doing the same things you've always done and expect change.

Willingness comes first, then action. If you're willing to make the changes you want to make, you're halfway there. Taking action requires commitment. Making this commitment to hold yourself accountable (to your community or family) is an excellent way to ensure you follow-through.

You don't always have to be the best. Strive for progress over perfection. The most important thing is that you gain enjoyment, fulfillment, or growth from the experience. If you become the best along the way, well, that's a bonus.

It's rewarding to see yourself improve at your sport or hobby. So set yourself up for success by accomplishing Specific, Measurable, Action-Oriented, Realistic and Time bound goals. (S.M.A.R.T) Don't be too hard on yourself after failure moments. You will not always achieve everything you target. Accountability can make you uncomfortable. Building mental toughness happens when you challenge yourself to get outside your comfort zone.

Set Long-term Goals

The best way to challenge yourself is by setting goals. Goals are a necessary component of growth because they help you track progress, build confidence, and stay motivated.

You can start your goal setting by thinking about your wildest dreams. As an athlete, what is your grand dream? Where do you want to end up? Beyond your sport, what kind of life do you want to lead? What would your life look like if you had no limitations? If you could magically eliminate all barriers to your success, where would you be and what would you be doing?

Create long-term goals based on what you want your sports career and/or your life to look like. Then, set short-term goals that support and lead to these long-term goals. Setting these short-term, process-focused goals enables you to build a pattern of success. A large part of mental toughness is framing your process correctly by setting SMART goals.

There is nothing wrong with dreaming big, but remember that you have to build a path to get there. That path should comprise realistic steps that will move you towards the bigger dream goal. Unrealistic goals are less likely to help. Start small and work your way up from there.

How to set S.M.A.R.T. short-term goals:

1. Make your goal **specific**. For example, instead of, **I want to get more hits or I want to get faster,** you can use, **I want to increase my batting average to .350 or I want to decrease my split time by 10 seconds.** When goals are vague, it's really difficult to determine if you actually succeeded. A short-term goal that is not specific is not helpful in achieving your long-term goal.

2. Set **measurable** goals. **I want to get better or I want to be a good golfer**, is not a measurable goal. My **batting average will increase by 25 points or I will play a complete round with a score of 74 or less** is. Ensure that you have some sort of metric to help you determine whether you've met the goal.

3. Set **action-oriented** goals. Focus on what you want to happen versus what you don't want to do. If I tell you don't think about a pink elephant, what happens? Our brains don't have a mental picture for **don't or not doing something**. For example, if you stay up too late playing video games and it's affecting your performance, using the goal of **don't play video games** is not an action. Instead, phrase your goal as the replacement behavior or action you will take instead. **I will go to bed at 10:30.** Instead of **don't strike out** use **hit well with 2 strikes** or **don't waste time at practice** use **stay focused and work hard.** Phrasing your goal as an action you can take makes it easier to accomplish.

4. Setting **realistic** goals is important as well. I will bench press 400 pounds, may be a realistic goal for some. But if you are a young athlete weighing 120 pounds. It is probably not. Your goals must have some stretch or challenge in them, to move you forward and help you grow, but they need to be possible for you in your current state or level of ability. As you improve, increase the challenge.

5. Setting **time bound** goals is critical. An open-ended goal with no time pressure for completion leads to procrastination. I want to lose weight is a dream. I will lose 2 pounds within the next 7 days is a time bound goal. A goal with no due date gets lost on your schedule of priorities.

Supercharge your goals by speaking them aloud to your support team. This makes goals real and holds you accountable. Your support team can not only remind you of your commitment if you stray, but they can root for you and cheer on your completions.

Acknowledge your effort. If you don't meet a goal one week, consider it an excellent opportunity to practice productive self-talk. When you achieve your goals, no matter how small, celebrate! Eat a favorite snack or watch your favorite movie or episode of a favorite TV show.

Tell your community, and they can celebrate with you. Progress won't always happen in a straight line. There will be difficulties as you pursue your goals. Even if you aren't seeing immediate results, remember that it takes time. Trust the process, put in the work, and you will make progress.

Your goals should be driven by your values. This helps you tap into internal motivation, which you will need during the long haul of goal pursuit. What are the things you value most? How can you live by those values?

Live According to Your Values

Using values as a guidepost is a great way to motivate yourself toward your goals. Under stress, our minds don't think clearly. Internalizing a set of core values provides the internal guidance you need during times of stress, confusion, and decision-making.

Your values help you determine how you want to live your life or train for your sport.

For example, if you value your community, you may invite your friends over for dinner once per week. Or if you value learning for its own sake, you might read interesting books or watch a documentary over comedy on Netflix. Or if you value trying your best at everything you do, you are more likely to keep trying, even if you've had a few setbacks.

By having a consistent set of values, you are moving towards consistency and meaning in your life. Values promote self-motivation and confidence. Life is more fulfilling when you know what's important to you and then align your actions with your values.

Values can help when you don't have a clue what to do.

For example, if you are considering two travel teams. Team A is far away, but higher ranked. You would need to spend two hours per day in the car to get to and from practices. Team B is lower ranked, but is much closer to home. If you/your parents value being on the best team, no matter the sacrifice of time, choose the first team. Whereas if you/your parents value having a more balanced life, you might choose the second team. Having a clear understanding of your values helps you make these hard decisions.

As a teenager, many decisions concerning your sport might not be yours alone. It will depend on your family situation, finances, etc. Clear values about the type of player, friend or teammate you want to be will guide the decisions you need to make. Having a set of core values will positively affect your entire life. People without values are easily influenced and can be led astray to poor life decisions.

Values are a concise guide to living your life.

When visualizing your values, it's important to visualize what they look like in action. It's one thing to value kindness, but it's another thing to use that value to help you treat others respectfully when you don't want to.

For example, the value of bravery might involve learning to speak up when you're nervous or taking responsibility for your behavior. The value of safety might look like putting on your seatbelt every time you get in a car. You may wake up early to work out if you value hard work.

Discover Your Values Drill

Follow this process to determine your values:

1. Begin by making a list of things you value (at least 10 things). Write them as a full sentence (My Family should come first) vs just a single word (Family). Think about how you try to live your life. What principles do you hold? How do you think you **should** act? How **should** people treat others or handle problems? What values do your parents, coaches, and mentors think are important? What is most important to you, your family, faith, fitness or financial success? Create your list to help you figure out what values matter to you.

2. Next, shorten that list to 3 - 6 values that are core or central to how you live your life (or want to) and begin visualizing them in your daily life.

3. Write each value down and put them somewhere where you see them each day (your mirror, desk, bedroom door or wall, gear bag).

4. Refer to your values often, and check-in with yourself to see if you're living up to them. If you stray, refocus onto your values without judgment or negative self-talk.

Setting your values helps during times of stress, because they give you a guideline for how you would like to live. Before you make any big decisions, pause in a moment of mindfulness and consult your values. They often offer a stronger perspective to make the best decision possible in any situation.

Personal Story

In high school, I had clear goals. I wanted to earn a college scholarship to play softball, and I wanted to be valedictorian. Depending on the year, this helped me figure out my short-term goals relative to those overarching goals.

Each year in softball, I had certain statistics (batting averages, on-base percentages, etc) I was shooting for. My SMART goals involved how many times a week I would practice (outside of team practices) or lift weights, and so on. These SMART goals changed if I was in or out of season.

For school, my short-term goal for each semester was straight A's. To get more specific for specific projects and tests, I had to consider the impact on my grade in each class. I calculated how many AP classes I needed to take. I made sure I did well in those classes, because they added more points to my GPA.

During the years my dad was my travel ball coach, he started every season by explaining his core values and how they were essential to our success. He still uses these core values today in everything he does. And I have incorporated them into my approach to life in my own way.

1. Do the right thing even when you don't feel like it.

2. Treat everyone as you want to be treated, even when they don't deserve it.

3. Strive to be excellent at all times in all things. The world does not need more mediocrity.

Players who didn't buy in to these values didn't make the team. Or they didn't stay on the team for very long. A well crafted set of core values helps you align yourself and your Championship Support Team with a higher purpose.

During high school, my values were based on my parent's values and we crystallized these values into our own slogan that kept us aligned and heading in the right direction.

Our slogan became; **Play Hard, Have Fun, No Mercy**. This slogan was part of our pre-game ritual. And we still remind each other often to live up to our slogan.

In my family, this goal of striving for excellence included the classroom and the field. Giving a weak effort was not acceptable. Quitting on your team or yourself was not acceptable. Treating other people poorly was not acceptable. Failing to educate myself about how to improve was not acceptable. Failure to do well in school was not acceptable. And doing something unethical or dishonest was not acceptable.

Knowing that these were the principles and standards that I would be held to in my home, the choices I made day-to-day were made in order to live these values to the best of my ability. This is how values drive the right actions.

In my case, if I couldn't play hard and enjoy the competition, whether I won or not, then I had to adjust my mindset. The other team is trying to win as well. No-one wins all the time. Losing is no excuse for berating officials or being a jerk around your family and friends. So for me, **Play Hard and Have Fun** helped me to enjoy improving my skills and overcoming failures.

And while **No Mercy** may seem a little mean, it has to be understood in context and what it meant (still means) for me. If I play hard and have fun, playing with focus and drive, the **No Mercy** mantra will not show up as cruel, mean or unsportsmanlike behavior. Treating people right, doing the right thing, and striving for excellence always took precedence, for me. **No Mercy**, is a phrase for me that sparks the competitive drive to never back down and never quit. My opponents deserved to receive my best effort so that they could grow and learn too.

These values definitely affected my life, especially in high school. They guided me as I pursued my athletic goals. They helped me stick to it when the days got tough, even when I didn't want to do the work. I am no longer a competitive athlete, but these core values are still essential to my life. Your values may shift over time as you experience life, and that's okay. But having clear principles to guide you is key to success, and a huge part of building and maintaining mental toughness.

Chapter Nine
Quick Fix Mental Skills You Can Use Now

The strategies in this book so far are long-term strategies that will help you build your mental toughness when applied consistently. If you continue to use them, you will improve your confidence and trust in your abilities. You will enhance your ability to be calm at any moment. You will improve your ability to be clutch under pressure and in the big moments of your sport.

Sometimes athletes need a quick fix to get through a currently tough time. These quick fix tools are the equivalent of mental toughness duct tape. These temporary fixes will buy you the time and space to do the proper work needed to fix the issue. Below are three quick fix strategies that will help you be Confident, Calm and Clutch in the moment.

Take a Deep Breath

Controlling your breath is one of the few ways to manipulate your physiology intentionally. You can use breathing to calm your body and mind down, to help you manage emotions, and refocus on what's important now. When you can take a big, slow, deep breath, it unlocks some very specific benefits during stressful performance moments. It helps you maintain precision, accuracy, and motor control. It enhances memory and recall (remember your game plan), sustains composure, primes concentration and mental agility, and improves reaction time.

The basics of deliberate breathing are to:

- Breathe Deep - breathe through your diaphragm into your belly. Act like you are blowing up a balloon inside your belly. This forces you to use your full lung capacity and helps slow your body down.

- Rhythm - pick a rhythm that works for you. This will take a bit of experimentation, but find a cadence or rhythm your body responds to. One rhythm is to breathe in for a count of 4-5 seconds, then exhaling for 4-5 seconds. You could also breathe in a box rhythm, when you breathe in and hold it for 4 seconds and then breathe out and hold it for 4 seconds each. You could breathe in for 4 seconds and exhale for 7. Each of these ways has research to back their effectiveness. It's important to figure out what works for you. *(see resource page for breath trainers)*

- Mental state - Let go and center yourself. Our thoughts drive our emotions and reactions. In order to help the breath be effective, it's important to quiet your mind. If you continue to think ineffective or unhelpful thoughts, it will work against the natural calming effect of the breath. Pick a neutral or calming thing if you can't quiet your mind completely. Consider using a simple work or phrase like **breathe, woosah, chill, quiet,** as a focal point.

Deliberate Breathing Drills

1. Daily Practice -Deliberate breathing is something you should practice regularly in order to train your body to engage the calming response. Build breath practice into your day-to-day routine. Pick a time and place that you will devote 2-3 minutes

to practice your deliberate breathing. Focus on breathing low and slow. Play with the different rhythms above to discover which works best for you.

2. Get Your Heart Rate Up- To practice using your deliberate breath under stressful conditions, spend one minute getting your heart rate up with some form of exercise (jumping jacks, run in place, burpees). The exercise mimics what it feels like to be nervous in a big moment. When the minute is over, start taking slow, deliberate breaths. The goal is to get your heart rate back down as quickly as possible. The bigger goal is to be able to reduce your heart rate back to normal within 2-3 breaths.

Refocus Technique

No matter how Confident, Calm and Clutch you are, you are still human and will have moments of distraction or counterproductive self-talk. Even if you proactively fill your brain with effective thoughts, doubts, worries, fears, distractions will still pop into your head. The goal is to get back on track quickly by refocusing. In order to do this, you will need to have a pre-planned strategy. Use the **AIR technique** in any situation where you need to regain your focus or get your thoughts back to being purposeful, productive, and possibility focused.

A–Be AWARE. To use this tool, you need to know that you need it. Tune into your thoughts. Are they creating confidence or a sense of certainty in your abilities? Are they focused on what's most important? If not, you need to use the rest of the technique.

I–INTERRUPT. The goal of this step is to stop the flow of your counterproductive thoughts. There are many ways to interrupt. It's possible to say stop, refocus, quiet or something similar. You can create a mental picture of a **stop sign**. Or run a mental video clip of Doctor Evil saying **Zip it** to Scotty (just go watch Austin Powers, this will make sense after that). You can use a physical action like **wiping the dirt with your cleats, bending down to pick up grass, tapping your foot, clapping your hands**. It could even be a big, slow, deep breath. The goal is to interrupt the flow of negative thoughts.

R-REPLACE. Now that you have broken up the flow of your thinking, you can replace your distracting thoughts with something more productive. A simple cue word or phrase can help you refocus on the task. Or, this could be a specific sport related cue like, **see ball hit ball, light feet, where's the puck?** You could ask yourself, **What is most important right now?** You could also use one of the **Critical Self-talk Drills** to reframe your thinking.

Refocus Drills

1. Sustained Focus Drill–You can practice this while doing any sport related task or even your homework. Build your **AIR** plan before you start. Then set a timer for 5 minutes. During that time, anytime when you get distracted, use your planned **AIR** technique. You can even pre-plan some distractions, have a parent or friend purposely try to distract you during that 5 minutes.

2. Trash Talk Competition - Pick a sport specific drill you can do with a parent or friend. Pick a drill that has a measurement to see how well you are doing it. (In one minute how many times can you...hitting balls off a tee to a specific location in the cage, making free throws, spot passing, taking shots on goal, given 30 attempts how many times did you make the shot, etc). You and your friend/parent should perform the drill once to determine your baseline score. Then, during your second attempt, have your friend trash-talk you or try to distract you in any way that doesn't prevent you from actually performing the drill (they can't steal the ball or block the goal). Use the **AIR** technique to stay focused or to fight back against counterproductive thoughts. The fun part is that you will switch places with your friend/parent. Whoever performs closest to their baseline score on the second attempt wins the game. This is fun because even if you have different skill levels, you are actually trying to beat or match your own previous score, not the other person's score. Making your mental toughness training fun is also a great way to ensure you will stick with it.

Pre-Performance Routine

One of the quickest ways to improve performance is to make sure you have a pre-performance routine. Consistency breads consistency. Pre-performance routines are a valuable tool for athletes. Having a deliberate routine helps you lock in your attention, helps you get your emotions and energy in the right place, and solidifies your confidence. By preparing for your performance in the same way, every time you are taking deliberate steps to control the aspects of your play that are within your control.

A pre-performance routine should start within 20-60 minutes of your performance, depending on what sport you play. You should have a pre-performance routine for the entire game/competition to ensure you are ready and prepared to compete in the game/event. It is also important to have a pre-performance routine for smaller performances within your sport (getting ready for an at bat, shooting a free throw, taking a penalty kick, hitting a serve or making a putt).

An effective routine ensures your thinking is productive, your body is under control, and your focus is on the right thing. Your pre-game routine should be flexible enough to adapt to the unexpected. (there was traffic and you are late, weather delay, the other team switched something up to affect your team's warm-ups, injuries and needing to get treatment before starting). Your routine should get you both physically and mentally ready to play.

As a team sport athlete, what does your team do to prepare? Can you insert your own personal preparation into the process? If you are an individual sport athlete, design a routine that works for you. You may need to incorporate breathing and refocusing exercises into your physical preparation routine.

For your smaller performances like a pre-shot routine, you can be a lot more specific. You can do it the same way every time. This routine might change over the duration of your sports career. My "getting into the batter's box" routine looked very different when I was 12 than it did my senior year of college. It needed to change because I was a different player by then and had different needs. You will adapt and change your routine during your career, but in any single game, it should always be the same.

Routines create comfort and familiarity. The more comfortable and familiar you are with the task, the easier it will be to control your thoughts, emotions, and behaviors. It can also unlock muscle memory to help you execute automatically.

There is no specific "DRILL" to help you build a good routine. You may have to experiment with a few ideas. During my softball travel team years, I discovered that pitchers always tried to get me out by pitching me low and outside. Therefore, the last drill I would perform before each game became taking 20 swings off the batting tee, with the ball placed low and away. This routine reinforced the muscle memory I needed to drive that pitch hard to the opposite field. This not only improved my batting average, but caused the pitcher to alter her game plan. You and your Support Team will need to find the routine that works best for you and your sport.

Being intentional about what you do before your performance is all it takes. Test routines out during practice to figure out what works for you. Your routine should include a combination of the physical and mental steps you need to feel ready to compete. Keep tweaking and experimenting until you find the right steps and thoughts that help you feel Confident, Calm and Clutch. If you are struggling to figure out what works for you, consider getting more help from me. *(See resource page for options)*

Chapter Ten

How to Fix Common Problems

This chapter covers several of the common problems young athletes face as they try to become Confident, Calm, and Clutch. The goal of this section is to help you address specific problems using the lessons from this book. Their categorization lists the most common mental toughness problems athletes face as a Confidence, Calmness or Clutch related issue. If you don't see your problem listed here, you can get more targeted help from me in the resources section.

With any problem you face building your mental toughness, there is one basic process you must follow in order to fix it. It is the fundamental process to enable change in any area of your life and is essential to becoming Confident, Calm and Clutch.

Here is the process:

> 1. **Discover** the barrier. What is preventing you from being Confident, Calm or Clutch? Is it your thoughts, your emotions, your behaviors? Are internal or external factors the issue? Is it a lack of skill or ability that is holding you back? Discovery requires you to **get curious and be honest without judgment.** The discovery process might require you to get input and feedback from your Champion Support Team. But once you

understand what is going on, then you can move onto build.

2. **Build** the skill. The process here is to build whatever skill you need to address the barrier you've discovered. This may be a physical skill you need to develop (something technical or sport specific). It could be a mental or emotional tool you need to build. You might have a mindset shift you need to make. Or you may need to change a negative behavior in order to get better. Use **SMART goals** (pg 66) to build a steady plan for improvement in that area and maintain Effective Self-Talk as you go through the process. Remember, change can take time. Trust the process and focus on progress, not perfection.

3. **Apply** the skill. Once you have worked to develop the skill, ability, or behavior that you need to address, you must now apply it. Commit to using the new skill, ability, or behavior in games and competitions. You should see changes in your results.

This is a cyclical process. You will have to re-engage in this process often to produce a lasting improvement. We are complex. As you grow and develop, you will discover additional barriers. That's okay and normal! You will set yourself up for success if you return to this process.

That's it! That's how simple the process is. Of course, simple doesn't mean easy. Making change is hard. Developing a new skill (physical, mental, or emotional) is hard. But you can do hard things.

Use the skills taught in this book to help you maintain a healthy mindset as you engage in this process and rely on your Champion Support Team to help you out along the way.

Confident

Problem 1: How do you become more confident? Do you constantly doubt yourself?

- Get Curious Drill Chapter 4 page (Paperback page 30)
- I Can't Drill Chapter 6 page (Paperback page 47)
- Self-Praise Drill Chapter 6 page (Paperback page 47)

Problem 2: How to bounce back after a mistake? If you make a mistake, it can snowball out of control. How can you get back on track?

- Refocus Technique Chapter 9 page (Paperback page 73)
- Ground Yourself Chapter 3 (Paperback page 25)
- Three Good Things Chapter 3 (Paperback page 27)

Problem 3: Do you constantly compare yourself to others? Does it damage your confidence if they are better than you are? How do you fix this? The goal is to focus on getting better as an athlete, not comparing yourself to others.

- Three Good Things Chapter 3 (Paperback page 27)
- Refocus Technique Chapter 9 (Paperback page 73)
- Set Goals based on values Chapter 8 (Paperback page 64)

Calm

Problem 4: Do you get so worried about making mistakes you lose focus and don't play well? How can I learn to become calm when I play?

- Deliberate Breathing Chapter 9 (Paperback page 72)
- Ground Yourself Chapter 3 (Paperback page 25)

- Reframe Drill Chapter 3 (Paperback page 23)

Problem 5: Do you find it hard to focus when you are nervous?

- Deliberate Breathing Chapter 9 (Paperback page 72)

- Visualize Your Emotions Chapter 3 (Paperback page 30)

- Refocus Technique Drills Chapter 9 (Paperback page 73)

Clutch

Problem 6: Are you inconsistent? Do you play well some days and play poorly on other days?

- Pre-Performance Routine Chapter 9 (Paperback page 75)

- Get Curious Chapter 4 (Paperback page 30)

- Consistency Drill Chapter 4 (Paperback page 33)

Problem 7: I can perform during practice, but when I get in a game, I freeze up. How do I handle pressure better?

- Mindfulness Drills Chapter 3 (Paperback page 25)

- Reframe Drill Chapter 3 (Paperback page 23)

- Pre-Performance Routine Chapter 9 (Paperback page 75)

Problem 8: I feel so much pressure to be perfect, like I'm going to let my team / parents /coaches down if I don't do well. How do I relieve the pressure?

- Communication Drill Chapter 5 (Paperback Page 39) If someone on your Support Team is causing you to feel this way, you might need to have a conversation to help them understand the impact they are having on you. The extra pressure they are putting on you is not intentional. They aren't doing it on purpose. They just need feedback from you. Everyone on your team plays a role in your success. Plan a time away from the playing field to have a check-in. Consider avoiding discussing issues pregame or post-game when emotions and anxiety are the highest. We don't do our best listening or communicating when emotions are high.

- Best Friend Drill Chapter 6 (Paperback page 47)

- Self-Compassion Drills Chapter 6 (Paperback page 51)

These are the eight most common problems athletes ask me about. However, there are certainly more that will affect your ability to be Confident, Calm and Clutch. If your issue isn't addressed here, check out the resources pages for more ways to get specific help from me.

Chapter Eleven
Conclusion

With everything you need to improve your mental toughness right here, it's time to pass on your love for your game and show other readers where they can find the same help. Simply by leaving your honest opinion of this book on Amazon, you'll show other athletes where they can find the information they're looking for, ready to improve their own skills and pass their passion for the sport forward. Thank you for your help. The game is kept alive when we pass on our knowledge – and you're helping me to do just that.

Leave Review

Conclusion

Life is rarely perfect, and sometimes it's wildly chaotic. Life is always beautiful. Being mentally tough will help you remember that through good times and bad.

Practicing these skills will strengthen your ability to bounce back from the curve balls that life and your sport can throw your way.

Keep these tools in mind and apply them to all areas of your life. Changing your thinking and behavior will strengthen your relationships with others, with yourself, and with the world around you.

Things can feel out of control without these skills. You may not feel mentally tough, but you are. Using these skills consistently and regularly will help you build your mental toughness and ability to thrive.

First, it's important to understand mental toughness.

Mental toughness isn't something you were just born with. You can develop mental toughness through training. Part of being a human is facing life's curveballs. Part of being mentally tough is growing through those opportunities, rather than letting them keep you down and learning to thrive and enjoy life.

Developing mental toughness will help you learn from your mistakes.

Resilience is a Measure of Mental Toughness.

Mental toughness includes admitting sadness, anxiety, fear, doubt. It's okay to feel negative emotions. Sometimes, life makes us feel negative emotions. It's healthy to allow yourself to feel these feelings. What you do next is more important. The actions you take when you're having negative emotions set the tone for the next wave of opportunity.

When you practice mental toughness, you'll find more intrinsic motivation and feel more hope. The skills that go into being mentally tough are excellent for leadership, relationships, and self-compassion.

As you think about your thoughts and emotions, you'll become more self-aware. You'll feel empowered to build the life you want to live.

Develop Your Emotion Regulation Skills.

Despite how it may sometimes feel, you have the freedom to choose your thoughts and reactions to certain stimuli or events. It's important to understand that feelings and thoughts are not facts. The best way to work on changing your attitude is by simply noticing your thoughts and emotions.

When you find yourself in a negative emotional spiral, take a step back and reframe the situation. It's easy to fall into traps where we tell ourselves stories about the worst-case-scenario. If you find that you're lost in a negative assumption, try balancing out your negative thoughts with positive possibilities.

Part of being mentally tough is being able to sit with emotions. You may have negative emotions, and you're allowed to admit it when you do. You can have emotions without acting on them. Mindfulness skills are a great way to access calm in the chaos.

A helpful way to build yourself up is by adding to your positive memory bank. No matter how small, the more happy memories you have, the better. Getting out and doing something fun or reconnecting with what is fun about your sport is a great way to come out of your shell and increase good feelings. You can also practice gratitude, balance your thoughts, and explore your hobbies.

Take Responsibility For Your Path.

You have every bit of power to create the sport career and life you want to create. No matter where you are now, you can choose your next step. You can look at your life objectively to observe what could change, what needs help, and what you're proud of.

Begin by getting curious about your thoughts, emotions, and behavior. Look at your situation and examine if there is a role you played in this.

Sometimes it's hard to admit or hard to see. Taking responsibility requires humility.

If you want to change, begin making changes by making minor adjustments to your daily routine. By working these things into your morning or evening habits, you'll be better able to stick to them.

Set reminders that will go off throughout the day, so that you remember to practice mindfulness. You can also check in with your feelings and see what you can learn from each moment.

Cultivate a Championship Support Team.

Having a community strengthens mental toughness, because it adds so much meaning to life. A strong community increases feelings of purpose and strength. Having others who care about you deeply adds a sense of security to your life. Those we surround ourselves with make difficult things bearable.

There are many ways to build a stronger community with those you know and begin new relationships with those you don't know. Think about your community and how to enhance it. You can take part in activities with existing friends or join a club and try something new with a new group of people.

It's helpful to be authentic when you interact with others in order to build the strongest connections.

When you're communicating with those around you, there are a few things to keep in mind. Be aware of your body language. Having a receptive posture makes you more approachable. Active listening means engaging in the conversation, and it will let the people you care about know that you're there for them.

Use your community to hold yourself accountable. Having a support group surrounding you will lift you up during difficult times and celebrate with you when times are good.

While you're trying new things and setting new goals, use your community to keep you aligned with the way you want to live your life.

Strengthen Your Relationship With Yourself.

Self-compassion is the key to mental toughness because it prioritizes your relationship with yourself. Taking care of yourself isn't selfish. Loving yourself isn't selfish. By giving yourself the care and attention you need, you'll nurture all forms of growth.

A vital part of self-compassion is preventing critical self-talk. Begin by observing the negative phrases you tell yourself daily. Once you notice what you say to yourself, work on coming up with balancing thoughts that are positive and reaffirming. Praise yourself for your hard work and willingness to change.

Give yourself permission to love yourself. Choose a self-compassion activity that works for you and make it a regular part of your life.

Get Your Body In Motion.

Exercise is an excellent remedy for both mental and physical health. Physical benefits are boundless. Psychological benefits are also a huge part of exercise. By creating new neural pathways in the brain and releasing feel-good chemicals, exercise is a natural medicine for mental health. It eases anxiety, depression, stress, and other distressing issues. Confidence and feelings of self-worth increase with exercise. Remember this as you train and take part in your sport.

Challenge Yourself.

Building mental toughness starts with you. Your mental toughness starts when you take action. Moving forward means you need to take the first step.

When you feel empowered over your life, you can take any action you need to create the life you want to live. Challenging yourself means encouraging yourself to pursue your full potential.

Setting goals pushes you to strive for what you're capable of. Believe in your best and go for it. Start by thinking of your wildest dreams. Set up some long-term goals and then start with short-term goals. Short-term goals are valuable stepping stones. Set goals each week to help move you forward.

Values Light The Way.

You can use your values to give you guideposts that will lead you toward the life you want to live. If you can imagine what your values look like in action, you can follow those actions. When making a crucial decision, always consider your values.

Following these seven steps will help you build your mental toughness and find a strength that you never realized you had. It will set you up for success in your sport and success in life.

I hope you found value in this book. This book, however, just scratches the surface of mental toughness training. If you would like more detailed training about how to build your mental toughness, please visit the Resource Section and check out the opportunities I offer.

Please review my book and tell me what you thought. I appreciate your honesty and look forward to helping you continue your journey along the path to Mental Toughness. Also please consider sharing this book with anyone else in your circle that might need it.

Chapter Twelve

Additional Resources

You can access the options discussed below by scanning the QR Code at the bottom of the page or by going directly to the Toughness Trainer App. You can download the app at no charge from your respective app store or access the web version by going to toughnesstrainer.passion.io (QR Code below).

Self-Awareness Tools

1. **Free Mental Toughness Journal PDF download.** This journal aims to help you build on the mental processes that help your performance, and discover what's getting in your way so you can change it. The first few pages of the journal explain what types of things you should be journaling about as it relates to your performance. The rest of the pages give you an opportunity to rate the quality of your confidence, motivation, focus, and energy each day. This allows you to see trends. The notes page allows you to reflect and think about your experiences that day, and how your specific thoughts, emotions, and physiological states affect you and your performance. You can print as many pages as you need to keep track of your progress.

2. **Physical Copy of the Confident, Calm & Clutch Mental Toughness Training Journal.** This has the same content and structure as the free download but is a 120 page journal

that doesn't require you to print repeated copies of the journal pages. The advantage of the physical journal is that all your pages and notes are bound and less likely to get misplaced. By purchasing the physical copy, you also get access to a FREE Mini-Course to help you learn more specific tools to help with your mental toughness.

3. **Take the Free Athletic Coping Skills Inventory.** Discover the areas of mental toughness that you need most help with. You can prioritize developing in the areas that you score the lowest. This should start having a positive impact on your performance.

Mindfulness Tools

1. **Toughness Trainer App** - Mindfulness is part of how I teach mental toughness. Many of my programs include recorded mindfulness practices in the training material. I also have a specific mindfulness section of my app, which includes instruction and guided meditations, to incorporate into your practice. Mindfulness is the pathway towards gaining better self-awareness, better emotional control, improved concentration and so much more. Consider downloading the app and getting started today. Some of the mindfulness practices are free, but the more robust training requires you to buy individual programs or a subscription.

2. There are many other apps on the market today to assist you with mindfulness practice. Just search mindfulness in your app store and plenty will show up. There are too many for me to list here. Most require a paid subscription.

3. There are also free apps for deliberate breathing training I use in my work with the Army that are pretty handy. They require little education, and they provide a guided breathing practice to help you improve your relaxation breathing. They are called Breathe2Relax and Tactical Breather. If you want more help with choosing the right tool, you can shoot me an email at **valerie.alston@valstoncoaching.com**

Webinars / Live Classes / Podcasts

1. I often run webinars and live classes throughout the year. These webinars run from 1 to 3 hours. Sometimes I hold a full day boot camp. These are great opportunities to learn more about mental toughness and practice the skills in a concentrated way. If you would like to receive notifications and updates when these opportunities are available, please use the link below to sign up for my mailing list.

2. I also have several webinars that I have recorded and make available to everyone. I often rotate these free recorded webinars, so I won't list them all here. But the link below will always show you the current offerings available.

3. I have been a guest on a few podcasts talking about my book or other mental toughness topics. These are often great opportunities to pick up a few additional tidbits on being Confident, Calm and Clutch. (use link below)

Online Programs

My on-demand programs are delivered through the Toughness Trainer App. This app is for personal remote coaching of young athletes trying to improve their mental game in order to reach their goals. (earning a college scholarship, becoming a sponsored player, making a national team). Use this personal coaching app to become a mentally tough athlete. If you want to be someone who competes hard, knows how to deal with failure moments, is coachable, and excels on the field and in life, then download my app. My focus on young athletes is intentional. You have the most to learn and can benefit the most from my training. Mental Toughness is critical to success in any walk of life.

All of my Mental Skills courses or challenges are appropriate for athletes middle school aged or older. As I am continually adding to my library of mental toughness courses, the list below may not be comprehensive. You can always get an up-to-date list of offerings from the link below.

1. **Mastering the Mental Game** - Learn specific mental tools to master your motivation, attention, confidence, and energy. Instantly increase the quality of your play and competitiveness by learning the tools to recover quicker from slumps, to handle pressure like a champ, and to deal with the natural difficulties of the game/sport. I designed this program for any level of athlete who wants to better manage the mental side of their sport.

2. **Confidence Kickstarter** - I help your athlete build their confidence so they can play with more joy and freedom. They will learn how to kick-start confidence by: (1) Eliminating doubt and fear so they can play free and with more joy; (2) Grow from failure and become truly resilient; (3) Perform at their highest potential consistently.

3. **Badass Ballplayer 6 or 12 Week Challenge** - I specifically designed this course for softball and baseball players to become Confident, Calm and Clutch. They can choose a condensed 6 week version with daily lessons and tasks, or the more casually paced 12 weeks version. The content is exactly the same. A

Badass Ballplayer is Confident, Calm and Clutch under pressure. They compete hard, know how to deal with failure moments, are coachable, and excel on the field and in life. They do all of this while also being a good teammate. I teach them the foundations of the mind-body connection to build self-awareness, how to improve their confidence, how to minimize nerves, focus fundamentals, how to fight their fears, and how to put it all together to perform consistently well under pressure.

4. **The Mental Edge Maximizer** - This is my comprehensive mental skills training program. I help elite high school athletes gain a mental edge and build the resilience needed to perform and thrive at the next level. In this program, I help you transform into the college athlete you want to be by learning about the Mental Edge Formula, which helps you:

1. Improve performance by building mental toughness and gaining the mental edge over others.

2. Be "recruitable" by becoming the type of athlete the college coaches want to invest in.

3. Learn valuable life skills that will serve you throughout your life, not just in sport.

I designed this program for elite athletes ages 13-18 looking to compete at the next level. You can sign up for 6 months or a year of access. It **includes weekly group coaching** and resilience training to help you deal with life outside of sports as well as sports psychology.

Personal & Group Coaching

1. **Private coaching sessions** - will be one-on-one with Valerie Alston via Zoom. I am trained in behavior change and motivational techniques. Rather than acting as the expert and giving advice, I will create an environment that gives you permission to take the lead. I adhere to what you want, not what I think you should want. You determine your unique goals through a process of self-discovery and accountability, and I facilitate change at a pace set by you. The goal of these sessions is to give you personalized coaching and help you apply the techniques in this book to build your mental toughness.

2. **Group Coaching** - As part of **Growth Club**, you can attend weekly group coaching calls. These sessions allow you to put the techniques you're learning in programs into practice during group coaching sessions. This is a safe place where everyone is working on their own Mental Toughness journey. These sessions allow you to ask questions about any of the content you have watched or the unique struggles you are facing as you play your sport. Most athletes find it powerful to learn that others are having similar struggles as them and to hear the creative ways they are showing up for themselves and creating solutions. Access to Growth Club requires a monthly subscription.

3. **Training the Trainer (For Adults Who Coach Young Athletes)**- If you want to become a more successful coach and help the athletes on your team thrive, I can work with you in a variety of ways. If that interests you, go to my website to learn more. Or send me an email at valerie.alston@valstoncoaching.com

Quick Links to all Resources

Toughness Trainer App

Index

- Calm Drills ... Chapter 9
- Champion Support Team ... Chapter 4
- Clutch Drills ... Chapter 9
- Communication Drills ... Chapter 4
- Confidence Drills ... Chapter 9
- Consistency Drill ... Chapter 3
- Critical Self-Talk Drills ... Chapter 5
- Deliberate Breathing Drills ... Chapter 8
- Discover Your Values Drill ... Chapter 7
- Get Curious Drill ... Chapter 3
- Gratitude Drill Chapter ... 2
- Mental Toughness Myths ... Chapter 1
- Mindfulness Drills ... Chapter 2
- Pre-Performance Drills ... Chapter 8

- Refocus Technique Drills ... Chapter 8
- Reframing Drill ... Chapter 2
- Self-Compassion Drills ... Chapter 5
- Set SMART Goals ... Chapter 7

Coaches Corner

After reading Confident, Calm & Clutch many coaches have asked me how to get copies of the book for every member of their team. Therefore I have developed a way for you to buy copies at a discount if you plan to use the book as part of your training regimen. Buy scanning the QR Code on the next page you will be able to buy the books for roughly a 33% discount off of the regular price.

In addition many coaches have reached out seeking guidance about how to implement mental skills training into their practice plans. So I have decided to develop a resource to help coaches deliberately and systematically implement these lessons into their coaching. The goal is to get this guide written and published by July of 2023. The coaching companion guide will provide several specific ways to help you implement Mental Toughness Training for your team. By scanning the QR code you will also have the opportunity to get on the wait list so that I can notify you when the new publication becomes available.

Mental Toughness training is the missing link when it comes to building athletes with the ability to compete at the highest levels. Please reach out and let me know if you have any questions or any ideas about what you would like to see included in the coaches guide to creating a team full of Confident, Calm and Clutch performers.

If you would like to learn more about how to order the book in bulk and get expert advice on how to use this book with your team please scan the QR code below for more details.

Made in the USA
Coppell, TX
23 April 2024